Praise for *THE GRE*

"It is better written than most scholarly books, more tightly researched than most books by journalists, more intelligently understood than books by people who have not themselves been part of the industry, and fairer-minded than much of the polemical literature on the politics of oil."

David Prindle author of *Petroleum Politics and the Texas Railroad Commission*

"No other industry, I dare say, boasts such colorful characters as the oil and gas industry. Cargill's meticulously researched book carries the reader from the earliest discoveries in Texas to later events such as the Arab oil embargo that struck at the core of our nation's economy. Seeking to understand the role and motivation of his father, who despite his foibles, was an inspiration to the author and others, Cargill exposes the intense rivalries between "little" oil and "big" oil, and how this tension encouraged Texas' notorious political chicanery. The Texas oil heist has only before been told as a footnote. Perhaps because the notoriety of the families whose fortunes were built through thievery was something better swept under the rug like the awkward uncle at Thanksgiving. Cargill's meticulously researched book shows why Texas and the oil industry have been and continue even today to be both envied and reviled."

James N. Falk President, World Affairs Council of Dallas Fort Worth, Dallas, TX

"Who would have thought a book about slant-hole drilling, even the illegal kind, would be interesting and enjoyable, much less a very good read? Bob Cargill has accomplished all of those things in his *The Great Texas Oil Heist*. He has done so in an accessible manner and with solid evidence. Highly recommended!"

Don Carleton, Executive Director of the Dolph Briscoe Center for American History, U Texas at Austin

THE GREAT TEXAS OIL HEIST

by

ROBERT CARGILL

STEPHEN F. AUSTIN STATE UNIVERSITY PRESS

Printed in the United States
All rights reserved.
First Edition

Production Manager: Kimberly Verhines

Cover design by Forbes & Butler Visual Communications
Cover photo: Railroad Commissioner Bill Murray speaking at the dedication of
the Boy Scout well on January 14, 1949.

IBSN: 978-1-62288-402-5

For more information:
Stephen F. Austin State University Press
P.O Box 6100 SFA Station
Nacogdoches, Texas 75962
sfapress@sfasu.edu
www.sfasu.edu/sfapress
936-468-1078

Distributed by Texas A&M University Press Consortium
www.tamupress.com

To Martha
who supported this work with love and affection

TABLE OF CONTENTS

It was 1946. World War II was over. The thieves went to work. They drilled deviated wells from outside the East Texas Oil Field back into the oil that remained after 16 years of production. This was the oil field that supplied the oil needed for an Allied victory in 1945. The deviators continued their nefarious activity until an angry and aggressive attorney general led his posse of lawmen, including the Texas Rangers, into East Texas to stop the theft and administer Texas justice.

I tell this story on the basis of 35 years of research and my father's well files. Yes, he drilled six of the nearly 400 deviated wells.

I first learned of the so-called Slant-Hole scandal in late spring 1962. That's when colleagues in my research group at the University of California at Berkeley accosted me with the morning's *San Francisco Chronicle*. They knew my father was an East Texas oilman. One pointed to an article reporting that oilmen in East Texas had drilled "deviated" oil wells from beyond the known productive limits of the East Texas Oil Field to steal oil.

"Has your dad been stealing oil?"

"Of course, not!" I replied.

I had known nothing of the illicit activity until that morning.

Then a report in *TIME* further exposed the East Texas oil scandal that had erupted in my hometown of Longview. (1)

In July of that year, my appointment at Berkeley ended. I drove to East Texas to spend six weeks with my parents in Longview before moving in September to my new job on the chemistry faculty of the University of South Carolina in Columbia. While I was in Longview, I learned that my father had drilled six of the 380 illegal wells, a revelation that shocked and greatly dismayed me. Like several of those who drilled the offending wells, my dad had drilled more than a hundred legitimate oil and gas wells in East Texas, and he had made a pile of money in so doing. Why get involved in this nefarious activity?

I found slant-hole drillers and their friends openly discussing the slant-hole matter, even on the post office steps. I avoided participating in these gatherings because I was seen as an outsider. At least one noted, "He's been at Berkeley, you know, that hotbed of Communism. That's ruined him."

I could tell, however, that there was a general animosity among locals toward Big Oil, the Railroad Commission, and Texas Attorney General Will Wilson, all of whom were seen as enemies of the hometown boys.

I debated with myself about what I should be doing with my six weeks in Longview: preparing my course in organic chemistry for my first teaching job, designing my first independent research program, or learning about the slant-hole matter? Any one of these could have occupied my full attention that summer. Every beginning assistant professor in a research university understands the "publish or perish" policy, one that I support. My future career depended on my academic preparations, so I decided to concentrate my efforts on my teaching and research responsibilities and let Dad deal with his own problems.

During my days in Longview I worked on what I planned for the fall in South Carolina, but in the evening my parents and I enjoyed playing games of moon—a three-handed version of the domino game "forty-two"—and drinking a little Jack Daniel's whiskey.

The phone rang and interrupted our game at about 10 p.m. on Saturday, August 18, 1962. Dad went into the bedroom, answered the phone, spoke briefly, and then reappeared.

"Pauline," he said, looking at the floor and still standing, "get your clothes together. We're leaving now."

I wondered why the sudden urgency to leave late at night. I got up and followed my father. I watched him take 10 one-thousand-dollar bills from a safe hidden under the floor of a downstairs closet. He knew I was there, but neither of us spoke. He may have had a bag with a change of clothes already in the car. Before he and my mother drove away, Dad said to me, "We're probably going to Caddo Lake and do some fishing. We might be away for a few days." Then he and my mother disappeared into the humid Texas night.

Caddo Lake is a cypress swamp of about 25,000 acres sited across the Texas-Louisiana border through which runs the Cypress Bayou. Almost no one ventures onto the lake after dark for fear of being lost among the cypress trees dripping with Spanish moss or meeting one of the lake's many alligators and/or water moccasins.

I knew he kept his fishing tackle, outboard motor, and paddles in the trunk of his car, so the fishing story might have been credible under other circumstances. But it was clear by the way my father got the money from the safe and so quickly left after the phone call that something was amiss. I knew, however, that further questioning about what was happening would not be welcomed, so I waved as they drove away and went to bed.

I awoke from a sound sleep to the ringing of the doorbell at 8 the next morning. At the front door I found a seven-foot giant with a chiseled face and piercing gray eyes. He was wearing a 10-gallon Stetson, had a .45 on his hip, and had the signature Cinco Peso Badge of a Texas Ranger displayed on his white shirt. It was 35-year-old Texas Ranger Glenn Elliott, late in his first year as a Ranger, who stood before me. We introduced ourselves, and then he got right to the point.

"Is your dad here?"

"No, sir. He got a phone call late last night and shortly thereafter he and my mother left, saying they might be going fishing at Caddo Lake."

The Ranger nodded, smiled, and looked down at his boots, as if he knew what I'd said was a cover story. Then he suggested that I ask my father to contact him when he got back. After that, Ranger Elliott wished me the best and left.

Perhaps I told Ranger Elliott more than might have been prudent. But I was a young man of 27, and when he looked into my eyes with his steel-gray eyes, I believed at that moment that he saw my entire soul. His presence was sufficiently intimidating that I would have told him far more than he needed to ask. At that moment I imagined what a captured suspect might have felt when an angry Ranger Elliott began to question him.

My parents returned the next Thursday. I learned then that the Saturday-night phone call had come from a mole in the attorney general's office. He warned the deviators that on Sunday morning Texas Rangers would serve subpoenas demanding their appearance at a Texas House General Investigating Committee hearing to be held in Dallas on Monday, August 27. Most (but not all) of the deviators heard from the mole directly or indirectly.

Not wishing to be found, my father and the other deviators assembled late on that Saturday night at the Washington Youree Hotel in Shreveport, Louisiana, beyond the reach of Texas lawmen. Well, maybe not legally out of reach, but the Rangers made little or no effort to find them. They partied there for four days. Someone kept tabs on the activities of Attorney General Will Wilson just to be certain there would be no further surprises before their inevitable return to Texas. Nobody expected to completely avoid the hearings, though. When my father came home, he called Ranger Elliott in my presence with an invitation to serve the subpoena.

My parents and I went to Dallas on Sunday, August 26. The first of five House General Investigating Committee hearings on the slant-hole matter was scheduled to begin the next morning with Representative Charles Ballman chairing the session. About 100 men had been subpoenaed to appear. This group included deviators as well as personnel of major oil companies, well-servicing companies, and the Texas Railroad Commission.

Chairman Ballman gaveled the hearing to order at 10 a.m. on Monday, August 27. Attorney Fred R. Erisman Jr., representing many of the suspected deviators, immediately challenged the jurisdiction and validity of the House committee. Rep. Ballman retorted, "Mr. Erisman, this House committee was not organized to go into the question of the legality of itself." With that dismissal, the hearing began. (2)

I recall little of the substance of the hearing other than the fact that most of the witnesses, who were deviators, refused to testify, claiming Fifth Amendment protection from self-incrimination. My father was not called to testify at this first of five hearings. But at the second hearing on September 10, he also refused to testify.

I met several of the deviators after the first day of hearings. A group of them, including my father, went to dinner at a swanky restaurant. My mother and I also attended. Some were friendly and likeable (Jake Maxwell), and some were insufferable (Harry Harrington and Jack McCubbin). McCubbin got drunk and asked my mother for a dance, but I intervened with some vigor. I was surprised to hear very little about the hearing there. Perhaps my presence was regarded as unwelcome, but no one spoke openly around me. This was an occasion in which my father was unusually tight-lipped; he did not speak of the matter while I was in his presence.

I left Texas a few days after that first hearing and spent the next 18 years totally absorbed in my own career. I gave no further thought to the slant-hole matter or my father's participation in it. Although I was never a famous scientist, my career at Carolina was satisfying. My 40 publications were generally regarded as good journeyman science, adequate for my being given the Russell Award for Excellence in Scientific Research by the university in 1974.

In February 1980, I celebrated my father's 71st birthday in Longview. During that visit he asked me to leave my teaching position and return to Longview to help save his business. He thought he was nearing bankruptcy, which surprised me. He had developed a small, but successful business empire based on drilling legitimate oil and gas wells. The choice of retiring on an academic salary or saving a business that was worth several million dollars at the time was a powerful incentive to say yes. So, I agreed to come home and try to save the business.

I arrived with my new bride (number two) in Longview in early September 1980. Once settled, I found myself immersed in accounting, real estate development and management, exploration for and development of lignite deposits, and managing my father's extensive oil and gas interests. He was fully occupied trying to save his Longview Savings and Loan Association, but he was unsuccessful. It was declared insolvent in 1987. I had neither the time nor the energy then to discuss the slant-hole matter with him.

Dad died suddenly on September 23, 1986. He suffered his third heart attack after a weekend of duck hunting on the Gulf Coast. This was just about the time that I felt competent to manage his shrunken empire.

In the 1980s I found a collection of newspaper articles about the slant-hole matter assembled by my father's personal assistant, Pat Smith. I told my mother about the discovery, and she produced her own collection of slant-hole articles. After reading these collected articles, I discovered Dad's old well files and the report of the Texas House General Investigating Committee, also saved by Smith.

I knew then that I had the basis on which to learn and tell the entire story of the scandal that had been covered up for 30 years.

I asked several people in Longview about the slant-hole affair, but most of them refused to discuss the matter and urged me to forget about telling this story. I learned that the slant-hole matter had previously been written about in books and magazines from the 1960s onward—all of which I have read, I think—overlooked critical details of the larceny. Who started the slant-hole drilling? Why? Who was involved? Why did the matter end as it did?

Here, then, for the first time, I reveal the story of how a few dozen oilmen stole up to 20 million barrels from the East Texas Oil Field.

Although I have now had more than 35 years of experience dealing with oil and gas matters, I do not claim to be a real oilman. During this time, I have dealt in oil and gas leases, and I have participated in the drilling of more than 100 oil and gas wells, and too many dry holes. I have experienced, painfully, the myriad ways in which many operators often cheat their investors. Through my research of the slant-hole matter, I have gained an understanding of the history of East Texas and how the oil patch worked in the middle of the twentieth century.

Now I am eager to share what I have learned and to tell the truth of the slant-hole scandal—the circumstances that made it inevitable, who did what to whom, and how the matter eventually reached its conclusion. Much of what I reveal in this book has been the tightly guarded secrets of the families of the participants so that grandchildren can be kept from knowledge of granddaddy's scandalous behavior. But most of what I reveal here lies barely hidden in the public record. The slant-hole story is a significant piece of Texas history, and it must be told before no one is left to tell it.

NOTES

1. "Oil: Slanted Larceny," *TIME*, Vol. LXXIX, No. 24, June 15, 1962; http://www.time.com/time/magazine/article/0,9171,873651,00.html.

2. Texas Legislature. House of Representatives. General Investigating Committee. *Official report to the House of Representatives of the 58th Legislature of Texas*, Book, v.1, 1963; (http://texashistory.unt.edu/ark:/67531/ metapth5869/: accessed March 14, 2012), University of North Texas Libraries, The Portal to Texas History, http://texashistory.unt.edu; crediting UNT Libraries, Denton, Texas. Further references to this report are styled "HGIC Report."

Mother Earth had been setting the stage for the tragicomedy that I call *The Great Texas Oil Heist* for 240 million years. That's when Earth's single continent Pangaea began to split apart into the seven continents we know today. The North American plate and the European and African-South American plate began a separation that left behind basins. The East Texas basin filled with salty water that eventually evaporated to deposit the Louann Salt, a layer of salt 5,000 feet thick. By 115 million years ago (the Cretaceous period), a shallow sea—the Western Inland Seaway—covered the land from Texas to Alaska where it deposited limestones, shales, and sandstones atop the salt as the waters rose and fell. The tops of these layers of rock were generally horizontal unless they had been deformed by events after deposition. (1)

Under the pressure of these overburden rock formations, the salt or basement rock became plastic and occasionally penetrated through some of the overlying rock, but rarely reached the surface. When the molten rock or salt from below rose they produced what are called uplifts and salt domes, respectively. These uplifts and salt domes pushed the overburden layers not penetrated upward to drape over the uplift or salt dome as anticlines - inverted "U"s. Where penetration occurred, the rising rock or salt caused the adjacent rock formation to bend upward.

In what became East Texas, the primordial sea deposited the Buda Lime(stone) in deep water, then the Maness Shale in less-deep water, and then the Woodbine Sand(stone) in shallow water. The Woodbine served as the reservoir rock that would eventually contain the oil of the East Texas Field. Atop the Woodbine came the Eagle Ford Shale. After deposition of the Eagle Ford, the Sabine Uplift rose beneath eastern Texas and northwestern Louisiana, and tilted the eastern portions of these rock formations upward. While these rocks were exposed, erosion wore away the tilted layers before the sea returned and deposited the

Austin Chalk across the uplifted ends of the earlier rocks.

These processes left the Woodbine tilted upward at its eastern extremity and capped off by the Eagle Ford Shale and Austin Chalk above and the Maness Shale and Buda Lime below. Because the Eagle Ford and Maness Shales are made up of tiny grains of mud, they are impermeable and nonporous while the Woodbine, generally composed of large grains of sand, is porous and permeable. Fluids can flow, if slowly, through the Woodbine, but not the shales above and below. In its eastern extremity the Woodbine disappears as the two shales merge; the Woodbine ends in a pinchout where it can trap fluids—oil, natural gas, and water—as a stratigraphic trap.

At its western side, the Woodbine dips to a depth of about 8,000 feet before rising again to the west where it meets the surface—outcrops— between Dallas and Ft. Worth. There the Woodbine collects rainwater that fills its pores and pushes any oil and/or gas that collected in the east-side trap entering from the Austin Chalk and Eagle Ford Shale–source rocks. Seven billion barrels of oil as well as a large quantity of natural gas collected in the Woodbine trap and remained dormant under the pressure of the column of salty water to the west until 1930.

A similar set of geological events of more recent geological age created the Spindletop Oil Field, named for a 12-foot high hill on the Texas Coastal Plain near Beaumont, Texas. (2) The Louann Salt lies some 30,000 feet below the Gulf Coastal Plain where the pressure is immense, adequate to force semi-liquid salt to penetrate the overlying rock. Late in geologic time, many upward salt intrusions into the coastal plain occurred, and, in a process like that described above for the formation of the East Texas Trap, created traps around the stalks of salt. In the Spindletop case, where the dome is about one mile in diameter, the surface rock was lifted up about 12 feet to form an anticline trap above the salt dome.

Where did the oil that accumulated in these traps come from? The most generally accepted theory of the genesis of oil is that it arises from organic sources. The numerous invertebrate animals in the oceans have been living and dying for eons. The organic detritus falls to the ocean's bottom and is covered by sedimentary depositions. As the process continues, the temperatures and pressures rise and this material undergoes chemical transformations that lead to kerogen, a mixture of molecules that contain mostly carbon and hydrogen, along with some nitrogen, oxygen, and sulfur. Further "cooking" of the kerogen removes most of these latter elements and leaves hydrocarbons. At the temperatures and pressures found at depths of 7,000-20,000 feet, the hydrocarbons formed in the cooking are those corresponding to oil, and at depths greater than 21,000 feet, the pressures and temperatures are adequate to break down the larger hydrocarbons to methane, the principal component of natural gas. (3)

The hydrocarbons—oil and gas—migrated through "source rocks" until they arrived in a trap where they remained until they oozed to the surface where oil seeps have been known since ancient times, or until 1858 when the first "oil well" in North America was drilled in Oil Springs, Ontario, Canada. But it was Edwin Drake's oil well, drilled near Titusville, Pennsylvania, in 1859 that provided the basis for the oil industry. Most of the oil discovered in the United States between 1859 and 1901 was refined to kerosene that replaced whale oil and "coal oil" as fuel for lighting and laid the foundation of Rockefeller's Standard Oil fortune. (4)

James S. (Big Jim) Hogg was born in the East Texas town of Rusk in 1851, the son of a Confederate general who died of war wounds in 1862. He was an imposing figure at more than three hundred pounds, and he served as Texas Attorney General from 1887 to 1891. Texans elected him governor in 1890. He despised John D. Rockefeller's Standard Oil Trust and those "damn-Yankee" railroads, and he sought to forbid Standard Oil from doing business in Texas. (5) As governor from 1891 to 1895, Hogg pushed new laws through the Legislature that eliminated the control the railroads held over freight and agricultural rates by establishing the Texas Railroad Commission. He also prevailed on Texas lawmakers to prohibit out-of-state corporations from doing business in Texas. (6) This was Hogg's effort to protect the small businesses of Texas from those rapacious big businesses like John D. Rockefeller's Standard Oil Company and the railroads.

Although oil had already been found in limited quantities in Texas, as well as in other states, no one was prepared for what came next.

NOTES

1. The geology of the East Texas Oil Field is discussed in more detail by re-
nowned geologist Michael T. Halbouty in Clark, James A., and Halbouty, Michael T., *The Last Boom*, Random House, New York, NY, 1972, pp. 113-118.

2. The story of Spindletop is told especially well in: J. A. Clark and M. T.
Halbouty, *Spindletop*, Gulf Publishing Company, Houston, 1952; and J. W.
Linsley, E. W. Reinstra, and J. A. Stiles, *Giant Under the Hill*, Texas State His-
torical Association, Austin, 2002.

3. Metin Cakanyildirim, https://www.utdallas.edu/~metin/Merit/Folios/hy-
drocarbonGeology.pdf.

4. Daniel Yergin, *The Prize*, Simon Schuster, New York, 1991. See Chapter 1,
pp. 19-34, for a review of the development of the oil industry.

5. Robert C., Cotner, "HOGG, JAMES STEPHEN," *Handbook of Texas Online*, (http://www.tshaonline.org/handbook/online/articles/fho17), accessed June 11, 2013, published by the Texas State Historical Association

6. David F. Prindle, *Handbook of Texas Online*, "Railroad Commission," accessed December 10, 2017,http://www.tshaonline.org/handbook/online/
articles/mdr01.

"For Texans, the 20th century did not begin on January 1, 1901, as it did for everyone else. It began nine days later, on Jan. 10, when, spurting drilling pipe, mud, gas and oil, the Lucas No. 1 well blew in at Spindletop near Beaumont." That's how Mary Ramos opened her review of the Spindletop discovery.(1), (2), (3)

Pattillo Higgins established a brickmaking business in 1886. He went to Indiana in 1889, where he observed brick makers producing bricks of the same quality as his own—but more efficiently—by using oil and natural gas to fire the kilns. From Indiana, he went to Ohio and Pennsylvania, where he observed oil and gas seeps and mineral springs similar to those he knew near Beaumont.

Higgins thought, "Maybe there's oil back home at similar places."

One such place in Texas was Sour Spring Mound, a 12-foot rise on an otherwise flat coastal prairie pushed upward by a column of salt. Higgins read whatever he could find about petroleum and geology and concluded that the coastal salt domes would be just the right places for the accumulation of oil. He decided to drill a well on Sour Spring Mound—later Spindletop Hill. Try as he might, however, Higgins could not convince anyone that oil would be found on the Texas Gulf Coast, including Rockefeller's Standard Oil Company.

Higgins organized the Gladys City Oil, Gas, and Manufacturing Company in 1892 to test his hypothesis that oil would lie over and beside the salt domes of the Texas Gulf Coast. The company acquired 1,077 acres of land, and with it, the rights to any oil that lay below the surface. His acquisition included Spindletop Hill. Higgins tried to find investors for his drilling project on the hill. But in 1894 William Kennedy, the well-respected assistant to the Texas state geologist, condemned Higgins's ideas of oil being coupled with the coastal salt domes. Kennedy claimed that the Gulf Coast prairies were of too-recent origin to contain oil-bearing rock.

The earlier discoveries at Corsicana and Sour Lake, small as they were, created interest in Spindletop Hill. Higgins, who had money from his brickmaking business, and his partners in the Gladys City Company finally were able to hire the Savage brothers to drill three wells for them at Spindletop. These brothers from West Virginia had drilled three successful shallow wells (683 feet) at Sour Lake in 1895, which was reason enough for Gladys City to hire them. The Savages failed to complete the three wells at Spindletop because each of the wells collapsed. Higgins and his partners in Gladys City parted ways in a disagreement over the drilling contract. In the dispute, Higgins lost his small ownership in the company in 1898.

The standard method for drilling for water and oil at the time was the repeated dropping of a heavy chisel attached to a cable into the drill hole—the cable-tool method. Cable-tool drilling, the method used by the Savage brothers, didn't provide a way to prevent the internal collapse of the hole. Thus, the strata of quicksand through which the Spindletop wells had to pass always collapsed into the hole, preventing further penetration by the cable-tool method.

But determined men like Higgins never admit defeat. Better drillers or better drilling methods might save Higgins' plan.

Antonio Francesco Luchich (known in America as Lucas), born September 9, 1855, in Spalato (also called Split), Croatia, graduated from the Polytechnic Institute at Graz, Austria, in 1875. He spent three years at the Naval Academy of Fiume and Pola and received a commission as a lieutenant in the Austrian navy. His Slavic origin caused trouble with the German boys and induced him to come to the United States to visit his uncle in Michigan in 1879. He started to work in America at a sawmill, where his skills became obvious to management. His salary in America was considerably greater than that of an Austrian navy lieutenant, so Lucas stayed in the United States and became a naturalized citizen in 1885. He changed his unpronounceable name to Anthony Francis Lucas, as his uncle had already done.

With his background in European geology and mining, Lucas became a mining engineer who sought gold and silver in the America. He looked for iron in North Carolina, but instead he found the love of his life: Caroline West FitzGerald. She soon became his wife.

Lucas explored the salt domes of the Louisiana Gulf Coast in 1893 and recognized that they provided sulfur and some oil and natural gas, as well as salt. Lucas and Higgins had somehow heard of each other. They agreed in 1899 to collaborate in drilling for oil at Spindletop Hill. Lucas employed the rotary drilling rig he had used in Louisiana instead of a cable-tool rig. But the rig Lucas employed on the first Spindletop well was incapable of handling both the weight of the drill pipe and the necessary torque—the force required to turn the drill pipe from the rotary table on the rig floor while the bit digs into the bottom of the hole. At 575 feet, the hole collapsed. Lucas and Higgins didn't have enough money to continue.

After Lucas's requests for money had been turned down by several prospects, Dr. William Battle Philips, a geologist at the University of Texas, visited Spindletop Hill, and agreed with the Lucas-Higgins hypothesis. He introduced Lucas to John Galey, a wildcatting legend and partner of James M. Guffey's in the oil company Guffey and Galey of Pittsburgh. This pair had made a fortune developing oil fields in Kansas, in Oklahoma, and in Texas at Corsicana, but none of these was spectacular. They were low on cash in 1900 but recommended the Lucas project to the Mellons of Pittsburgh. The Mellons, Guffey, and Galey agreed to a deal with Lucas. But Higgins, the Mellons said, had to be excluded. I found no reason for the exclusion of Higgins other than a desire to keep the deal a secret among the greedy monied group: the Mellon brothers, Richard and Andrew, Guffey, Galey, and Lucas. Higgins did have a reputation for being difficult; when he was a teenager, he'd killed a lawman. That may have been enough reason for the Mellons. Lucas agreed. He was unwilling to share any of his one-eighth interest in the deal with Higgins. Now the Lucas group was ready to drill. Higgins had no further dealings with Lucas, even though Carrie Lucas tried to reconcile the two.

Guffey and Galey had worked with the three Hamill brothers at Corsicana and had recommended that Lucas hire them to drill their first wildcat well on Spindletop Hill. Jim, Curt, and Al Hamill had already drilled many wells in developing the Corsicana Oil field, discovered in 1894 when the town fathers, seeking water needed to develop the small town, found oil instead. The Hamills had learned to use a rotary drilling rig instead of the cable-tool method. Just as important, they learned that circulating mud down through the drill string (the pipes connected to one another for drilling), out the drill bit, and up the annulus (the space between the pipe and the hole's wall) had several advantages over circulating water to clean the hole as it was being drilled. These included sealing the surface of the borehole and, owing to the mud's greater density, bringing drill cuttings to the surface. They created the necessary mud by driving a neighbor's herd of cows into a pit of clay and water to stir the mess to the proper consistency. These improvements in drilling technique remain standard today.

Four dry holes drilled by others using the cable-tool method had already been abandoned, each the victim of a collapsed hole caused by heaving quicksand. But the Hamills began drilling operations (known as "spudding" the new well) using the new rotary method on October 27, 1900, just 49 days after a great hurricane destroyed Galveston, 68 miles southwest of the drill site.

More problems arose after December 9, 1900, and the Hamills were about to abandon the well when Carrie Lucas appeared. She explained to the Hamills and Galey, apparently, in language they understood, that the contract stated that the well would be drilled to 1,200 feet, and abandonment was out of the question. After a week of relaxation for Christmas, the Hamills started drilling again. At 960 feet, a yellow substance came to the surface that Lucas failed to recognize as sulfur.

The weather was bitterly cold and windy when the drill bit reached a depth of 1,100 feet on January 9, 1901. Shortly after daylight the next morning, Al Hamill was changing to a new drill bit. He had run about 700 feet of pipe, tipped with the new bit, back into the borehole when the rig shuddered, the earth rumbled, and then—amid a great roar and shaking of the rig—massive amounts of mud and rocks shot skyward through the derrick. The drill string followed the mud and rocks upward through the derrick and knocked off the crown block (the stationary part of the block-and-tackle assembly that allows raising and lowering the drill string) at the derrick's top. This was a small volcano, loud, scary, and dangerous. The flying pipe broke apart at its joints and fell earthward in pieces, landing with loud thuds. Then the scene was quiet—with occasional cheers—and there was no activity at the well from the early morning blowout until 10:30 a.m. Then oil rose faster and faster until it gushed 150 feet above the wrecked derrick at a rate estimated by engineers from Standard Oil to be about 80,000 barrels per day, making it the most prolific oil well ever drilled at the time. In fact, this was more oil than all the other producing wells in the United States combined had made. The Hamills finally capped the geyser of oil on January 19 after losing nearly a million barrels of oil that had spread over the surrounding prairie. Such a prolific oil well was unthinkable in 1901, and there was no provision for such a volume of oil. A workman on the scene coined a new term when he remarked, "Mister, that's some gusher, ain't it?" The Lucas Gusher ushered in the Age of Texas Oil that January morning in 1901.

In January 1901, shortly after the Lucas well at Spindletop gushed oil, former governor Hogg and Jim Swayne, a former state senator, created the Hogg-Swayne Syndicate as a vehicle for investing in Texas oil. They traded acres of land for shares of Texas Fuel Company, and the combine became The Texas Company on April 7, 1902. The company officially changed its name to Texaco in 1959, the name it had been called informally for many years.

By the end of 1901, Spindletop had spawned 440 gushers and had produced more than 3.5 million barrels of oil, 17.4 million by the end of 1902, and an additional 8.5 million in 1903. The Spindletop oilmen allowed wells to flow at their natural high rate and thereby allowed the native field pressure to decline too rapidly to maintain production over the long term. By 1904, only 100 of the 1,000 wells drilled on the hill produced at a rate of 10,000 barrels per day. And by 1907, the hill had given up nearly all of its original 50 million barrels of oil. There was almost nothing left. The original field was effectively depleted within a few years but was revived in 1925 when a new discovery at Spindletop was made at a depth of 2,588 feet in a deeper stratum.

The profligate oilmen had allowed their gushers on Spindletop Hill to spread oil all over the marshy coastal plain, wasting an estimated 10 million barrels in the first year of production. That oil accumulated in streams and lakes and was accidentally ignited on March 3, 1903. A giant fire ensued. Lucas ordered his men to establish a counter-fire east of the original blaze that stopped the conflagration in a giant explosion when the two fires met. Another fire erupted in April 1903 and destroyed 152 derricks on a tract owned by former Governor Hogg and his associates.

It wasn't long before chemists showed that Spindletop oil, selling at 10 cents per barrel, was not only a cheaper fuel than coal but was more efficient and more easily obtained and transported. Even at five times the going price, oil was a better fuel bargain than was coal.

Some 600 drilling companies came into existence at Spindletop during 1901. Many went broke and were never heard of again. The successful ones grew, merged, bought others, and were bought. In this process, Spindletop became the birthplace of Big Oil in America. Gulf Oil (formerly Guffey Petroleum Company, now Chevron), The Texas Company (later Texaco, now Chevron), Standard Oil of Indiana (Amoco, now BP), and Humble Oil (later Exxon) all grew out of the successful small ventures at Spindletop. (4)

The self-taught geologists Pattillo Higgins and Anthony Lucas were the visionaries who forced the drilling of the discovery well at Spindletop, but it was Big Money that reaped the big financial rewards.

Pattillo Higgins didn't disappear quietly though. He created his own Higgins Oil Company that completed the sixth gusher on Spindletop Hill. He continued to drill for oil in various Texas fields, but he usually moved on before the real money was made. He sued his former partners and was sued by them, ultimately settling the suits without disclosing who got what. At age 45 he married his 18-year-old adopted daughter, with whom he had two sons and a daughter he named Gladys. Higgins died on June 5, 1955, in San Antonio.

Captain Lucas never mentioned Higgins again and no information has come to light about the rift between them. He sold his interest in Guffey Petroleum back to Guffey and moved on to drill for oil in Mexico. He retired to Washington, DC, and spent the rest of his life working as a consulting engineer and traveling with Carrie. He died on September 2, 1921, in Washington.

James Guffey, the financial genius who persuaded the Mellons to finance the discovery well, allowed the Mellons to maneuver him out of Gulf Oil for $2.5 million.

John Galey, the wildcatting man with a nose for oil, died bankrupt in 1918.

The three Hamill brothers continued to drill wells together and then separately, and all three died as old men. Jim was 79, Al was 80, and Curt was 100. In 1952, Curt said, "Mr. Higgins, according to my idea, is the real man that found Beaumont or the Spindletop Oil Field, but it was developed by Captain Lucas. And I have never understood why Mr. Higgins has not gained more popularity through the early days and even up till now." Although most people still refer to the Lucas well, I agree with Curt that Higgins should have gotten the real credit for the discovery. It was Higgins's idea, but it required Lucas, Guffey, Galey, the Hamills, and the Mellons to make his idea a reality.

NOTES

1. I am unable to resist quoting Mary Ramos' introductory sentence to her review of Spindletop. Mary G. Ramos, https://texasalmanac.com/topics/business/oil-and-texas-cultural-history, Accessed April 2, 2018, RC

2. The story of Spindletop is told especially well by Clark and Halbouty, and by Linsley, Reinstra, and Stiles. I have summarized these accounts in order to show how the David and Goliath story is repeated over and over.

   a. James A. Clark and Michael T. Halbouty, *Spindletop*, Gulf Publishing Company, Houston, 1952.

   b. Judith W. Linsley, Ellen W. Reinstra, and Jo A. Stiles, *Giant Under the Hill*, Texas State Historical Association, Austin, 2002.

3. Jim Day chronicles irreverently what is known in Texas as the "Awl Bidness." He does not hesitate to name the liars and cheats whose names fill books about oil; but there's not a word about The Great Texas Oil Heist in his books on the American Oil Patch:

   a. James M. Day, Bridger House Publishers, Inc., Carson City, NV, 2002.

   b. James M. Day, *Oilmen and Other Scoundrels*, Barricade Books Inc., Fort Lee, NJ 2004.

   See also:

   c. James M. Day, *What Every American Should Know About the Mid East and Oil*, Bridger House Publishers, Inc., Carson City, NV, 1998.

4. These integrated oil companies and their successors are in oil patch jargon called Big Oil. The term Little Oil refers to smaller oil companies, especially the rapidly disappearing sole proprietorship oilmen, whose activities are generally limited to exploration and production of oil and natural gas.

CHAPTER 3
SPINDLETOP TO EAST TEXAS

After the 1901 discovery at Spindletop, drilling for oil became the *raison d'etre* for entrepreneurs and con men. Here was a means of getting rich quickly, and all such activities draw crowds rapidly.

By 1905, several drillers had found natural gas 825 feet below the surface in northwest Caddo Parish, Louisiana, near the eastern end of Caddo Lake. (1) This was the first time oil had come near East Texas. Then, in 1910, the Gulf Refining Company, the successor of Guffey Petroleum Company of Spindletop fame, leased 8,000 acres of the bottom of Caddo Lake at a cost of $30,000 to drill eight wells and drew up an agreement to pay $70,000 in royalties. In 1911, Gulf drilled the required eight wells on wooden platforms built of 140 cypress logs each, driven into the lake bottom near what became Oil City, Louisiana. The yet-to-be-discovered East Texas oil field lay only 60 miles west.

Caddo Lake has a maximum depth of 20 feet, with the average depth only about four feet; thus, the construction of the drilling platforms, while challenging, was made less difficult by the shallow depth of the water. Each well was a gusher. These were the first wells ever drilled offshore (not on platforms extending from shore) for oil. The first well, Gulf Oil's Ferry Lake #1, (from the earlier name of the lake) was drilled to a depth of 2,185 feet and produced 450 barrels of oil per day. (2) My father told me that in his youth he saw these wells flowing a solid eight-inch stream of oil.

No one except the Skippers of Longview suspected in 1911 that the Black Giant lay waiting to be found. The folks in Kilgore, Longview, and Henderson, however, wanted some indication that they, too, would be delivered from their bondage of poverty by the discovery of their oil.

The 29-year-old Barney Skipper quit his job selling men's clothing in Dallas and returned to his home in Longview in 1911. There he found work at the local haberdashery, Perkins Brothers, for $15 per week; but after six months he began to sell real estate. For several years Barney's father had been claiming, apparently with no credible evidence, that oil would be found in Gregg County if only someone would drill. Soon Barney joined his father in preaching the existence of a great ocean of oil lying under the farms just west of Longview to anyone who would listen. The people of East Texas, desperate for economic relief, listened to and believed in these oil evangelists even though none of them knew anything about finding oil. (3)

The year 1911 also saw the dissolution of the Standard Oil Trust. Ross Sterling, later governor of Texas, and other independent oilmen incorporated the Humble Oil & Refining Company of Texas. They named the company for the town of Humble, Texas, about 20 miles north of Houston where they had already drilled successful oil wells. Eight years later, Humble doubled its number of shares and sold half to Standard Oil of New Jersey, but the combined company operated in Texas as Humble Oil until 1964. William S. Farish, later president of Humble between 1922 and 1932, had been a pal of Walter Teagle's, president of Standard Oil of New Jersey, and it seems likely that the two concocted the Standard-Humble deal in order to break the state prohibition on out-of-state corporations. This sale to Standard elevated Humble Oil into the ranks of Big Oil. Humble's officers like Farish ceased complaining about Big Oil's predatory acts and became one of the most predatory. (6)

Roxana Petroleum Company, the drilling and exploration subsidiary of Shell Oil Company, had drilled a well in 1915 about three miles southeast of Kilgore, and had missed the eastern edge of the Woodbine Sand by a mile and a half. This dry hole just made the major company geologists more adamant that East Texas was without oil. Skipper continued his search for a driller anyway. (7)

By 1917, the Texas Legislature had stripped the Railroad Commission of its authority to regulate railroads, but assigned it the responsibility of regulating oil pipelines. The Railroad Commission, without a name change, would eventually regulate all oil and gas activity within the state. (8)

Small oil fields and some large ones had already been discovered in numerous places in Texas and in Oklahoma by the late 1920s, but most of Big Oil—Humble Oil, Pure Oil, Arkansas Fuel Oil, Sun Oil, Gulf Oil, The Texas Company, and Shell Oil—steadfastly insisted that no oil could exist in the piney woods of East Texas. In part, they reasoned that no subsurface anticline structure existed in East Texas. Standard Oil, forbidden to operate in Texas, seemed to remain on the sidelines.

J. Malcolm Crim of Kilgore, normally a conservative businessman and keeper of a general store in Kilgore, was the son of W. R. and Lou Della Thompson Crim. Lou Della's father, John Martin Thompson, had prospered, as had her husband. Mr. Thompson died in 1907, and when time for dividing his estate arrived, Lou Della eschewed the Thompson money and business and settled for the old family home and 900-acre farm. She and Mr. Crim had no need for more cash. Malcolm, Lou Della's eldest son, eventually took over his father's general store and became known as "the Sage of Kilgore."

Some time after his marriage to Kati Mai Birdwell on August 28, 1913, Malcolm and his new bride were in the spa town of Mineral Wells—the home of the Crazy Hotel and Crazy Water Crystals—to visit her parents. Malcolm was alone one day and found himself in front of a fortune-teller's tent. He entered, and for 50 cents, she told him, "You have a farm. It is bounded on the north and west by a creek. There is a railroad line running through it, and there is a big house on a hill. There is oil on your farm, and someday you'll discover it. There is oil on other farms bordering yours. You should get that land if you can." The description of the farm was accurate, and when she told him the initials of his neighbor, Malcolm concluded that he should find that oil. By 1921, Crim, on the strength of the fortune-teller's words, had leased 20,000 acres around Kilgore; but he couldn't induce anyone to drill and had to abandon the leases. Later he held 8,000 acres of leased minerals that he also abandoned for lack of interest on the part of drillers. But Crim was a man possessed. He never stopped trying to find someone to drill for the oil he thought was under his mother's land. (9) No oil company wanted to take the risk of drilling in East Texas even if Skipper's disciples believed desperately it was there.

Walter W. Lechner, the son of a farming family in Terrell had recently returned home from the battlefields of World War I. In 1920, Dr. Hugh H. Tucker, a family friend and respected geologist, invited Walter and his father to join him on a field trip in eastern Harrison County near the Louisiana border. On that excursion, Tucker examined the outcropping of lignite along the banks of a creek, collected a sample, and studied it thoroughly. He then told the Lechners that a great oil field would someday be found at relatively shallow depth about 45 miles west of their location, a little west of Longview. Walter was intrigued. (10)

In the early 1920s, Col. Henry Doherty, President of Cities Service Company—Big Oil—called for the unitization of all oil fields and for governmental control of production, because overproduction was forcing expensive storage of production in excess of market demand. (11) Storage in steel tanks was beginning to cost companies like Humble and Cities Service about 75 cents per barrel. Around the same time, in 1921, overproduction led to a drop in the price of crude oil from $3.50 per barrel to $1.00 per barrel. Thus, overproduction and the demand for storage cut heavily into the profits of all producers. (12) As the price of oil dropped, wildcat exploration became unattractive, especially when the evidence for the presence of oil was at best weak.

In 1923, the Texas Court of Civil Appeals denied a challenge of Standard's acquisition of Humble's stock by the Texas attorney general, and the Texas Supreme Court refused to hear an appeal. (13) With Standard's participation, Humble was the largest oil producer in Texas in 1925, and by 1929, it was the largest pipeline company in the United States. Humble and the other major companies – Big Oil - sought to control the production, transport, and refining of oil. They could ill afford to have others, such as Crim and Lechner—Little Oil—finding large deposits of oil that they didn't control. (14)

Lechner searched for another geologist who would corroborate Dr. Tucker's assertion about oil just west of Longview; but could find none. Dr. Tucker had proved his credentials as a geologist with his staking the location of the Santa Rita #1 well that blew in on May 28, 1923, and marked the discovery of the vast Big Lake Field in Reagan County. That oil field, along with other lands rich in oil, were part of 2.3 million acres of land granted by the state of Texas to the state university system in 1876 and 1883. Royalties from these lands have provided enormous sums of money for the University of Texas and Texas A&M University. (15)

Oil prospects in East Texas took another blow in 1924 when a wildcatter, Patrick White, without conferring with Skipper, drilled a well three miles east of Longview. Skipper would surely have told White to drill west of the town, but without Skipper's input, White drilled in the wrong place and the well was a dry hole. Many in Gregg County were discouraged, but Skipper continued his exhortations that oil lay beneath East Texas. (16)

Columbus Marion Joiner, who came to be known as "Dad", was already 60 years old when he came to East Texas in 1920. He was a man of almost no schooling but had taught himself to read and write from the Bible. He was many things: poet, charlatan, con man, and gambler, to mention only a few. Joiner could quote both scripture and poetry with a flair that made him especially attractive to older women. He had learned the trade of buying and selling oil leases, and had actually drilled some wells, all of which were dry holes. In fact, he almost discovered the Seminole Field in Oklahoma, but ran out of money when he had drilled to 3,150 feet where he abandoned the well. Empire Gas and Fuel Company (Cities Service Company) later drilled 200 feet deeper on a nearby lease and brought in the great field. (17)

Joiner made a living by buying leases cheaply and then promoting a greater fool to buy them from him at a profit. (18) He had purchased some leases in Rusk County in 1920 that he held without drilling for an extended period, but he eventually abandoned them for lack of drilling. He moved from Ardmore, Oklahoma, to Dallas in 1925, where he took advantage of the obituaries in the Dallas papers to find recent widows of wealthy men. After a suitable period of mourning he would ply his trade, inducing the widows to buy worthless leases. Joiner told a group at the Overton State Bank, "Every woman has a certain place on her neck, and when I touch it they automatically start writing me a check. I may be the only man on earth who knows just how to locate that spot." Then he added, "Of course, the checks are not always good." Thus he covered the costs of maintaining his family back in Oklahoma. (19)

On August 11, 1925, Joiner leased 580 acres of Daisy Bradford's 975.5-acre farm in the Juan Ximenes Survey about 10 miles south of Kilgore in Rusk County. Miss Daisy was an attractive lady at age 54. Her husband, Dr. William Bradford, had died on January 9, 1904, leaving her to live alone on the farm that she had inherited from her father, Dr. Henry Miller. (20)

Another con man, Joseph Edelbert Durham, who called himself Dr. A. D. Lloyd, a confederate of Joiner's from the Oklahoma days, had resurfaced in Fort Worth in 1927. Joiner was glad to find his old partner and induced him to provide a report and "geological map" that could be used in selling interests in his drilling venture.

Lloyd eventually produced his report on the prospects for finding oil beneath the cotton fields of Rusk County, along with a map of East Texas dated May 1927 and signed "Made for C. M. Joiner, May 1927 by A. D. Lloyd, Geologist and Petroleum Engineer, Fort Worth, Texas." The map showed four anticline structures, the Overton, the Johnson Creek, the Joiner, and the Lloyd Anticlines southeast from Overton and London. There seems to be no evidence of Lloyd's having had any formal training in geology or engineering, but he was a skilled promoter. He had changed his name because he had left behind a string of broken-hearted ladies (in spite of his 300-pound frame), demonstrating his skill as a snake oil salesman. Lloyd's 1927 "Report" predicted oil would be found on the Bradford acreage at about 3,500 feet. (21)

On March 19, 1927, Humble announced the success of an oil well drilled into the Woodbine Sand—the discovery of the Carey Lake (later Boggy Creek) field just 50 miles southwest of Miss Daisy's farm. But this trap was the child of a salt intrusion, and no such intrusions had been found near the Bradford farm. (22) And while Joiner was drilling his second unsuccessful well, the Daisy Bradford #2, in 1928, the Texas Company (Texaco) assembled an experienced crew with good equipment, and leased acreage south of Henderson. They drilled to a depth of 3,578 feet, but found no Woodbine Sand and no oil. The condemnation of East Texas was stronger than ever. (23)

By mid-1927, Miss Daisy was growing impatient with Joiner, whose lease payments were chronically late. He would cajole her, and because she had no other opportunities to lease her farm, she would acquiesce and their business relationship would continue.

At last, the Railroad Commission decided it must act on unitization. On April 24, 1928, the Railroad Commission unitized the Yates Field, discovered in 1926, in West Texas and established proration rules for production. With unitization, all operators had to cooperate, willingly or not, in the rational development of a field, and all stakeholders would share equitably the income from production. This rational method of development represented government control and was rejected by majors and independents alike, but when oil prices began to drop again in 1928, even Humble President Farish and the American Petroleum Institute decided to support unitization. If Big Oil was for it, the independents—Little Oil—were automatically against it. The independents asked, "If we have an oversupply of oil in the United States, why are you importing oil from Mexico and Venezuela?" Today, Texas remains the only state in which some form of unitization is not mandatory, a result of the animosity of the state's politicians toward the federal government and occasionally even toward state government. (24)

In the fall of 1928, Sir Henri Deterding, chairman of Royal Dutch Shell Group, hosted the following men at Achnacarry Castle in Scotland: Walter Teagle, chairman of Standard Oil of New Jersey (now Exxon); Colonel Robert Stewart, chairman of Standard Oil of Indiana (later Amoco, now absorbed by BP); William Mellon, president of Gulf Oil (now part of Chevron); and Sir John Cadman of Anglo-Persian Oil Company (now BP). Golfing and pheasant shooting were important activities, but there was serious business to be handled, as well.

These individuals knew the competition among them was leading to increasingly lower prices for too much oil. On September 17, 1928, they arrived at and signed a secret agreement they called the As Is Agreement of 1928. President Truman made public most, but not all, of its contents in 1952 after he decided not to run for re-election. That's when it became known as the Achnacarry Agreement. The substance of the Agreement was that each company would:

- Maintain its existing share of the world market.
- Not compete against the other companies.
- Share facilities and exchange oil so that it could be delivered by the shortest and least expensive route.
- Fix the price of oil outside the United States at the price of crude oil on the Texas Gulf Coast plus the cost of transport. (25), (26)

After the general principles of the As Is Agreement had been settled, the signatories entered into further agreements to define in progressively greater detail the functions of the local cartels established in consuming countries. These functions included fixing quotas, making adjustments for underproduction and overproduction, fixing prices, and dealing with outsiders—independent suppliers and refiners who were uninvited non-signatories to the Agreement. The point was that the outsiders had to be controlled either by buying them or ruining them.

John Blair wrote, "Not only would the development of an entirely new, and potentially very large, source of supply [of oil] have contravened such a recommendation [limiting production of oil not controlled by the majors]; it would have enormously complicated the task of setting up the domestic control mechanism" envisioned in the Agreement. "And," he continued, "accordingly, the development of an oil shale industry was stopped in its tracks by the Executive Order and by the closing of the Bureau of Mines' [two] pilot plants." (27)

Karl A. Crowley, a Fort Worth lawyer, testified before the Temporary National Economic Committee in 1939 regarding the 1926 discovery of the Great Permian Basin in Winkler County, Texas. He said, "There the majors had condemned that entire area as being worthless for oil—said that it was impossible to produce oil from the formations that were found there. It was condemned as being so utterly worthless that the foolhardy wildcatter there was unable to sell any of his leases to the major companies." (28) That same Permian Basin continues to be a prolific producer of oil and new discoveries have made it America's most prolific. The early condemnation of East Texas, followed by the great discovery, reminds that prejudice is often counterproductive.

On October 13, 1929, Pure Oil Company completed its discovery well in the Van field in Van Zandt County, about 60 miles west of the Bradford location. It was another Woodbine field. That meant that the oil was again found in the Woodbine Sand; but this field is "on structure." At Van, the Woodbine develops an anticline in which the oil is trapped at the top with water pressing upward from below. The important issue related to the Van field was its voluntary unitization by all operators in 1929. The operators, Pure, Humble, Shell, Sun, and Texas Company, agreed to allocate interests in the production among themselves according to leased acreage. This arrangement allowed the operators to develop the field rationally and in concert, rather than to drill more wells than necessary, to secure maximum advantage for themselves indirectly. (29)

The people of East Texas held a grudge against Big Oil because of their conviction—based on the ravings of the Skippers and the promotions by Joiner and Lloyd—that the major companies had increased their suffering in poverty by denying the existence of oil in East Texas and by their adversarial relationships with local drillers—Little Oil.

Joiner found a motley crew, an old drilling rig, and some rusted pipe. With an inauspicious beginning, his driller, Tom Jones, commenced to drill—or, "spudded"—on Miss Daisy's farm in May 1927, as recommended by Doc Lloyd.

Alas, by the time he reached a depth of 1,098 feet in February 1928, the pipe was stuck and could not be moved up or down. Joiner abandoned the well and Jones went to work for Gulf Oil in Venezuela.

On April 14 of the same year, with the rig moved just a hundred feet to the west, Joiner and his crew spudded the Daisy Bradford #2 well. A year later, on April 28, 1929, Joiner' driller, Bill Osborne, abandoned the second well in disgust. The drill pipe had "twisted off" when he reached a depth of 2,518 feet. (30)

Joiner's new driller Ed Laster and his crew began to skid the fragile rig toward the west on May 8, 1929, but they had moved the rig only 375 feet when the skid broke. Laster determined to drill a third well right there; he spudded the Daisy Bradford #3 on the spot. By late March 1930, he had reached a depth of 2,640 feet when the rotten drill pipe twisted off.

Miss Daisy was ready to terminate Joiner's lease, which was due to expire at midnight, August 10, 1930. She gave in at 11:58 P.M., but not until Joiner agreed that Laster would be in control of the third well. (31) After more arduous work and frustration, on September 5 Laster reached a depth of 3,536 feet where he did a drill-stem test that proved he had reached the Woodbine and oil. (32), (33) Late on Sunday afternoon, October 5, the Daisy Bradford #3 gushed oil at a rate of about 6,800 barrels per day. The East Texas Oil field had finally revealed a sliver of itself.

Joiner could hardly celebrate his great discovery; the con man had sold interests in his syndicates to finance drilling far in excess of 100 percent. In fact, certificates in Joiner's third syndicate, the Bradford #3 well, included entitlement to 4 of 320 acres in this venture, but Joiner had sold 300 such certificates, 220 more than were valid.

H. L. Hunt came to Joiner's rescue. On November 26, Hunt bought all of Joiner's interests—5,000 acres of leased minerals—including the 80-acre tract where the Bradford #3 was located--for a total of $1,335,000. Hunt paid the first $24,000 in cash; the remainder was to be paid out of Hunt's income from the Bradford properties he had just bought, if any. (34)

In short order, another three wells were drilled into the Woodbine: Deep Rock Oil's Ashby #1 flowed 3,000 barrels per day on December 13; Ed Bateman brough in his Lou Della Crim #1 at 22,000 barrels per day on December 28, 10 miles north of Bradford #3. A group that included Walter Lechner, Barney Skipper, W.A. Moncrief and Arkansas Fuel Company opened the F.K. Lathrop #1 16 miles farther north. All these wells produced from the Woodbine and demonstrated the new field covered an unusually large area. (35)

Of the first dozen wells drilled into the East Texas Woodbine, not one was drilled by a major oil company, a fact that wasn't lost on the people of East Texas. (36) Once the enormity of the new field and the potential volume of oil it contained became clear, Shell Oil, Sinclair Oil, and Humble Oil immediately came to East Texas to buy mineral leases. (37)

And the East Texas boom was on. The population of Kilgore exploded from about 800 to more than 8,000 almost overnight. Among the newcomers were fortune seekers of all sorts. My great-uncle Martin Hays, then sheriff of Gregg County, and his small crops of deputies were overwhelmed. That's when Malcolm Crim secretly arranged for Texas Ranger Manuel Trazazas Gonzaullas, better known as "Lone Wolf" Gonzaullas, to bring order to the new boomtown. And he did. When the local jails were full, he chained his prisoners to a "trotline" (a long steel cable stretched the length of the local Baptist Church.) (38)

NOTES

1. The lake now called Caddo had been called Ferry and Fairy in the 19th century. For a fascinating history of this now endangered wetland lake see Jacques Bagur, *A History Navigation on Cypress Bayou and the Lakes*, University of North Texas Press.

2. Bob Bowman, http://www.texasescapes.com/AllThingsHistorical/First-Over-Water-Oil-Well-BB1006.htm, accessed 4 10, 2018 RC.

3. The fits and starts that culminated in the discovery of the great East Texas Oil Field are well told by Clark and Halbouty (4) and by Clark (5).

4. James A. Clark, and Michael T. Halbouty, *The Last Boom*, Random House, New York, NY, 1972.

5. James A. Clark, *An Oilman's Oilman*, Gulf Publishing Company, Houston, TX, 1979.

6. H. M. Larson and K. W. Porter, *History of the Humble Oil & Refining Company*, Harper Brothers Publishers, New York, NY, 1959, Chapter 2.

7. Clark, p. 68.

8. David F. Prindle, *Petroleum Politics and the Texas Railroad Commission*, University of Texas Press, Austin, TX, 1981, pp. 19 & 20.

9. James M. Day, *The Black Giant*, Bridger House Publishers, Inc., Carson City, NV, 2002, pp. 11, 12. Clark and Halbouty, pp. 10 & 11.

10. Clark, p. 1. Tucker proved his credibility when he staked the location of the Santa Rita #1, the discovery well of the Big Lake Field in Reagan County in 1923. The Big Lake Field has provided more than $1billion in royalties to the University of Texas.

11. Clark and Halbouty, p. 146.

12. Larson and Porter, p. 180.

13. Ibid., p. 82.

14. John M. Blair, *The Control of Oil*, Vintage Books, New York, NY, 1978, pp.125 -127.

15. Clark, p. 80

16. Clark and Halbouty, pp. 13 &14.

17. Clark, p. 66.

18. In the oil patch, the operator, or principal owner, will often "promote" or sell interests in the project at such a profit that his retained interest covers his share of the costs, and often more.

19. Clark and Halbouty, p. 43.

20. Ibid., p 20.

21. Clark, p 58.

22. Clark and Halbouty, p 24.

23. Ibid. p. 32.

24. *Handbook of Texas Online*, Julia Cauble Smith, "Yates Oilfield," accessed April 23, 2018, http://www.tshaonline.org/handbook/online/articles/doy01.

25. Blair, Chapter 7, pp. 152-187.

26. James M. Day, *Oilmen and Other Scoundrels*, Barricade Books, Inc., Fort Lee, NJ, 2004, Chapter 11, pp. 137-144.

27. Blair, pp. 337.

28. Ibid., p. 160.

29. Clark and Halbouty, p. 150.

30. The rotary at the rig floor provides torque through the pipe to the bit at the bottom of the hole. Sometimes the resistance of the rock to the bit exceeds the strength of the pipe, especially old rusty pipe, and causes the pipe to twist in two; thus the term "twist off." The lower piece of the twisted off pipe could not be moved, and the well had to be abandoned.

31. Clark and Halbouty, pp. 59-61.

32. The drill-stem test involves an uncased hole filled with drilling mud. A packer—a device that can be expanded to the sides of the hole to make a seal, and that can be opened and closed to allow and disallow fluid to enter the drill pipe—is attached to the bottom of the drill string, closed, and lowered into the hole to a point at the top of the formation to be tested. The packer is expanded to seal off everything except the remaining hole below the packer. Once the seal is made the tailpipe is opened for a designated period of time, and oil, gas, and/or formation water that exists in the formation being tested will flow into the now opened drill pipe, provided the pressure of the formation is adequate. The packer is closed and the drill string containing whatever material may have entered during the test is removed from the hole. The amount of oil and water collected is reported as a function of time. Thus a drill-stem test (DST) might show that 3 barrels of oil was produced in 15 minutes of a DST.

33. Clark and Halbouty, pp. 49-59.

34. Ibid., pp. 92- 96.

35. Ibid., pp. 95-107.

36. Clark, p. 85.

37. Day, Oilmen, p.171.

38. Clark and Halbouty, pp. 135-140.

CHAPTER 4
THE EAST TEXAS OIL BOOM

By March 1931, Big Oil controlled the purchase, transport, and refining of most of America's oil. That put them in a position to carry out the aims of the Achnacarry Agreement of controlling world oil markets. With this in mind, the majors dropped the prices they paid independents for their oil to 67 cents per barrel, then to 35 cents, and then to 15 cents. In some cases the price got as low as two cents. These price reductions, not reflected in the prices of refined products such as gasoline, allowed the majors to maintain high profits. The independents responded by drilling more wells, which, of course, was counterproductive. The greater supply drove the price even lower, but Humble drilled wells even faster than did the independents. Big Oil had refused to consider that a giant oil field might lie under East Texas, but once the small wildcatters proved its existence, Big Oil entered with cash and muscle and bought almost half of the new field. Independents held on to the rest. Big Oil did not gain complete control.

Within nine months of its discovery, the East Texas Oil Field was producing almost one million barrels of oil per day. This volume of production, much of it beyond the control of Big Oil, frustrated the implementation of the Achnacarry Agreement and its control mechanisms, at least temporarily. Oil in the East Texas Field was being sold at the low price of 50 cents per barrel, but on April 24, 1933, the majors dropped the posted price to 10 cents per barrel in an attempt to convince independents to agree to prorationing—limiting the amount of oil produced in a given period. Big Oil had the advantage of both producing oil and refining it. Thus, the major refining companies were almost the sole buyers of oil produced by outsiders—Little Oil. Then "the majors said in effect, 'Cut your production in East Texas to what we think it ought to be and we will pay you $1.00 a barrel for oil. If you do not, we will ruin you with low prices.'" Big Oil "not only got enacted [by the Texas Legislature] the proration law, but also bought tens of millions of barrels of oil at from 10 cents to 50 cents per barrel." (1)

By 1932, the major companies were spending what cash they could find buying leases at sky-high prices. Major oil companies such as Amerada, Simms, Tidewater (later named Getty), Stanolind, and Sun became active around the Lathrop well, Gregg County's first producer, but Atlantic (later ARCO, and now absorbed into BP) started buying only after 500 wells had been drilled. Had the company listened to its Dallas geologist, Bob Whitehead, Atlantic could have had the entire Skipper-Lechner leasehold and much more for practically nothing. At a great cost, Atlantic eventually became the fourth-largest producer in the great new field.

On August 11, 1939, after the price of oil had recovered to one dollar per barrel, Humble cut its posted price for East Texas crude oil from a dollar per barrel to an average of 80 cents per barrel. At the same time, the U.S. District Court at Austin decided that Humble could produce 5,000 additional barrels of East Texas crude per day. The court's decision, coupled with Humble's cutting the price per barrel by 18 percent in a time of excess production, enraged the independent producers and the public in East Texas.

In response, Jerry Sadler, a Railroad Commissioner between 1939 and 1942, attempted to get Humble to reverse its price cut. Sadler, born near the East Texas town of Palestine in 1907, grew into a snuff-dipping, fist-fighting lawyer and was briefly a law partner of Fred Erisman's in Longview. He wrote to William S. Farish of Standard Oil of New Jersey (then a 50 percent owner of Humble) that "unless Humble either cut the retail price of gasoline (then at 8.7 cents per gallon) at least five cents per gallon, or restored the crude oil price cut, the 'Standard Oil Company' would stand convicted of having determined, through its 'Texas puppet company,' to rule or ruin the oil industry, to drive every independent out of business, to deprive the State of Texas of funds for the care of its blind and aged, to deplete the state's oil reserves for the benefit of the 'money barons of Wall Street,' or to turn control of the oil business over to the federal government." (2)

The Railroad Commission then ordered a 15-day shutdown of the East Texas Oil Field that quickly spread to Louisiana, Oklahoma, New Mexico, and Kansas. And when Humble's Harry C. Weiss testified before the commission that Humble's working stock of crude was far below its minimum level of 11–12 million barrels, the commission extended the shutdown for two extra days. Humble promptly rescinded its price cut retroactively, and the commission immediately terminated the shutdown. (3)

The people of East Texas believed the major oil companies had done them wrong. These outsiders failed to heed the con men's predictions that oil would be found in East Texas, leaving wildcatters to discover the field themselves with little encouragement from the big oil companies. Did Big Oil know oil lay beneath the farms of Gregg and Rusk Counties and refuse to drill in order to avoid the disruption of their plans developed at Achnacarry? Or did they really not believe oil was there? In the people's minds, it was the former. They felt Big Oil unnecessarily extended their poverty and deserved retribution. Now they hailed men such as Joiner as heroes. The people remembered how these determined gamblers—Joiner and the drillers of the first several wells that showed the extent of the new field—had struggled hard, with poor equipment and almost no cash, to bring in the greatest oil field the world had ever seen.

During the period between the discovery of the Black Giant in 1930 and the mid-1960s, the relationships between independent operators and the major oil companies deteriorated further. Issues such as well spacing, prorationing, pooling, and the importing of cheap foreign oil divided the two camps. The Railroad Commission's clear favoritism toward the independents prevented their growing hostility toward Big Oil from becoming violent. The logic of forcing owners of small tracts to pool with larger tracts, usually owned by the majors, could be swallowed if some concessions were made to the smaller players. When imported oil amounted to 12 percent of U.S. consumption in 1958, the majors reaped huge profits by selling Saudi oil (produced at a cost of 18 cents per barrel) for three dollars per barrel. Domestic oil, on the other hand, also selling at three dollars per barrel, cost the independents almost two dollars per barrel to produce, making their profits minuscule compared to those of the majors. The imports, along with increasing domestic production, forced the Railroad Commission to reduce the allowable production in

Texas back to eight days per month, further squeezing the independents and exacerbating their ill will toward the majors. (4), (5), (6), (7)

Hundreds of steel derricks sparkled in the sunlight of downtown Kilgore, Texas, for decades. As late as 1959, I walked among the 24 wells drilled in the 1930s on the "World's Richest Acre" on 10 separate lots by six different operators. These 24 wells produced a total of 2.5 million barrels of oil before the encroachment of water forced their abandonment. All the oil ever produced from that city block could have been produced with a single well instead of those 24, but greed overcame good sense. Each driller demanded the right to produce any oil he could find even if it meant less for everybody and damage to the life of the field.

The geology of East Texas may be fixed, but ill will and politics can be manipulated, and greedy men will always seek a fast buck. The figures below show the new field in cross section, aerial view of the original field, and the extent of water encroachment as oil was removed up to 1971.

Figure 4.1 shows an east-west cross section of the East Texas Oil Field. At its eastern edge, the Woodbine Sand shrinks in thickness to nothing in a pinchout where the upper and lower nonporous rocks—the Austin Chalk above, and the Maness Shale below—come together to create a seal. This depiction is a convenient oversimplification of the eastern edge of the Woodbine Sand but is adequate for understanding our story.

Figure 4.1: Schematic Cross Section, East Texas Basin

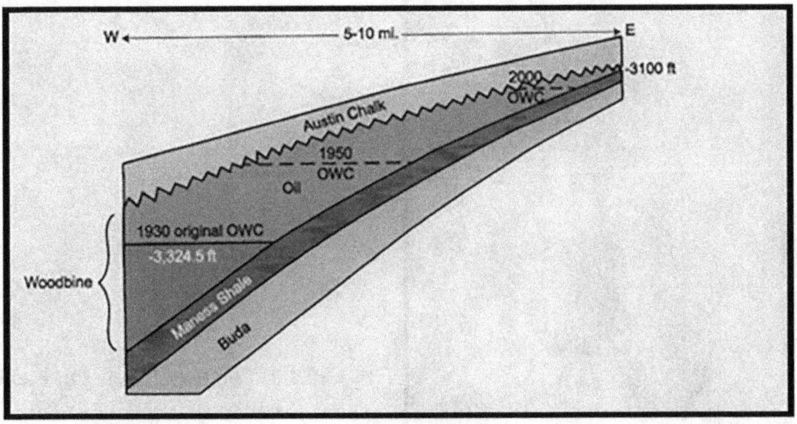

Source: Wang (2014, Figure 2, p. 51), used by permission of the Bureau of Economic Geology, University of Texas at Austin (OWC means oil-water contact.)

Figure 4.2 shows an aerial view of the East Texas Oil Field as discovered. It extended in rural East Texas 43 miles from its northern extent in Upshur County to its southern limit, barely extending into Smith and Cherokee counties, and averaged about five miles in width. Most of the original oil-in-place lay beneath Gregg and Rusk Counties. By 2014, the great field had produced 5.4 billion barrels of oil, plus a further unknown amount of unrecorded "Hot Oil." An estimated 1.6 billion barrels remain in the reservoir, and 70 million barrels are likely to be produced by 2030, according to F. P. Wang of the University of Texas, who reported on development strategies for the field in 2014. (8) By the end of 1939, a total of 31,580 wells had been drilled in the field; 25,829 of them had been drilled on tracts ranging from half an acre to 15 acres. By 2014, only 3,886 oil-producing wells remained (only 12 percent of the total drilled), and these producing at an average rate of 10 barrels per day. (9) All the other wells have been abandoned because the encroachment of water from the west led to the production of too much water and too little oil via these wells to be profitable. The number of producing wells continues to decrease.

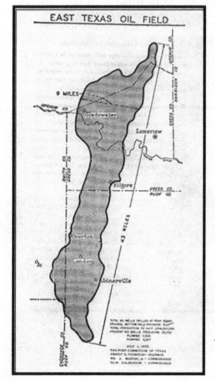

Figure 4.2: The East Texas Oil Field

Source: James A. Clark, Three Stars for the Colonel, p. 85. This is a product Railroad Commission, and is in the public domain. of the Texas

The Woodbine Sand, along with its upper and lower sealing rocks, dips westward from a depth of about 3,000 feet below sea level at its eastern pinchout to a depth of 8,000 feet. Then it turns upward, reaching the surface along a line roughly along Interstate Highway 35 between Dallas and Temple. Along its outcrop, the Woodbine collects water that fills its pores and closes the trap containing the reservoir's oil. This water also provides the pressure that drives the oil upward and eastward into the pinchout and into wellbores.

When oil is removed from the Woodbine reservoir, the column of water drives the remaining oil upward and eastward, moving the oil-water contact upward and the western limit of oil within the reservoir eastward.

Thus, wells that had been producers near the western limit of the reservoir now produce only water or have been abandoned. Oil produced from the eastern edge of the reservoir, on the other hand, is replaced by oil being pushed into its place by the water drive. The result is that owners of wells on the east side, where the original oil-in-place was the least, will see continued production until the very last of the oil has been removed.

Owners of wells on the west side, where the reservoir is the thickest and where the most oil originally lay in place, saw their oil removed by their own wells and by its being pushed eastward to replace oil produced from the east side of the field. Figure 4.3 shows this process.

Figure 4.3: Water Encroachment from Production of Oil (1930–1971)

Source: Staff, East Texas Salt Water Disposal Company, Salt Water Disposal, East Texas Oil Field, 2nd ed., Petroleum Extension Service, University of Texas Extension Service, Austin, TX, 1958.

NOTES

1. John M. Blair, *The Control of Oil*, Vintage Books, New York, NY, 1978, pp.160 -161.

2. H. M. Larson and K. W. Porter, *History of the Humble Oil & Refining Company*, Harper Brothers Publishers, New York, NY, 1959, p. 531.

3. Larson and Porter, pp. 529–535. The story of Sadler's attack on Humble, quoted here, is worth reading.

4. David F. Prindle, *Petroleum Politics and the Texas Railroad Commission*, University of Texas Press, Austin, TX, 1981, pp. 70–94.

5. Bryan, Burrough, *The Big Rich*, The Penguin Press, New York, NY, 2009.

6. For a brief review of the early days of the East Texas Oil Field and its troubles, see http://www.rehtwogunraconteur.com/the-big-oil-companies-are-strangling-the-very-life-out-of-the-industry/.

7. See James M. Day, *The Black Giant*, Bridger House Publishers, Inc., Carson City, NV, 2002, Chapter 13, "Big Oil v. Little Oil," for a discussion of the conflict between major companies and independents.

8. F. P. Wang, 2014, "Development Strategies for Maximizing East Texas Oil Field Production: The University of Texas at Austin, Bureau of Economic Geology, final contract report prepared for RPSEA" (Research Partnership to Secure Energy for America, Small Producers Program, under contract no. 08123-16, 83 pp.)

9. Ibid., pp. 5-7.

CHAPTER 5
HUNTINGTON BEACH

The excitement in East Texas was equaled by developments on the Southern California coast.

Mother Nature was generous with her hydrocarbon goodies. In addition to deposits in Texas and Oklahoma, she left billions of barrels of black gold in California. Thus, the Golden State was producing more oil than any other state in 1903. It wasn't until the discovery of the East Texas field that California's production fell to third. (1) Why discuss oil in California in a story about Texas oil? Because the events in Huntington Beach foreshadow similar events in East Texas some thirty years later although apparently few Texas oilmen read the California newspapers.

In Orange County, it was March 11, 1919, when Union Oil's Chapman #1 blew in at a rate of 8,000 barrels of oil per day, the most productive well in California at the time. (2) Standard Oil of California (controlled by the Rockefeller family) immediately leased nearby property and drilled six producing wells. Then, Standard leased 500 acres of Huntington Beach where its Huntington A-1 well found oil at 2,199 feet and flowed 91 barrels of oil per day from an oil zone at 2,379 feet on May 24, 1920. The new oil discovery catalyzed a population explosion in the little farming town, from 1,680 in 1920 to 6,000 by 1923. (3), (4), (5)

Between 1920 and 1927, wells produced oil from oil-bearing strata that lay about 2,300 to 4,800 feet below the surface. The more straws in a soda, the faster the drink disappears. Greed is the major characteristic of oilmen; the managers of Standard Oil were especially greedy. Too many wells too close together produced increasing volumes of oil between 1920 and 1926 when production fell from 26 million barrels from 594 wells to almost 8 million barrels from 355 wells in 1930 when the cumulative total was 181 million barrels. (6) Even by February 1922, the *Santa Ana Register* noted the foolishness of drilling of wells on small town lots (which are typically 150 ft. by 50 ft., meaning wells were 50 ft. apart) without further rules for spacing. (7)

From the water's edge, a beautiful sandy beach rises slightly toward Ocean Avenue (now the Pacific Coast Highway). The eastern limit of the beach meets a bluff at the western edge of the town. At some places the bluff is almost non-existent and at others it rises to about 50 feet or more. By 1927, production from the original group of wells had declined to almost nothing. That's when Standard Oil leased the "P. E. Strip", a ribbon of land 150 feet wide between the Pacific Electric Railroad that ran along the western side of Ocean Avenue and the beach. They built a retaining wall along the beach side of the bluff to prevent collapse of the bluff as well as their derricks. By 1930, all the land along the bluff on both sides of the street not occupied by railroad or street was covered with wooden derricks for about a mile. Photographs taken at the time show oil wells cheek-by-jowl between the bluff and the Pacific Electric Railroad and Ocean Avenue, and along the eastern side of the street. (8), (9)

Most of the drillers assumed their wells were vertically straight. They had no reason to believe otherwise.

Consider, however, that once the drill string (made up of 30-foot-long joints of steel pipe) reaches significant length, it will behave much like a wet spaghetti noodle. Try twisting a wet noodle at one end and controlling the other end; you can't. Thus, the turning (clockwise) bit will naturally lead the drill string along a downward spiral. When the bit encounters a change in the hardness of the rock being penetrated, such as when it crosses a fault plane, it will likely be driven further off course, and the driller will probably not realize the deviation. Such deflections of more than 500 feet were not uncommon.

At about the same time, three different groups, all in Huntington Beach—H. John Eastman, (10), (11), (12) Harold McVicar and "Doc" Rood (13), and Alexander Anderson (14)—developed methods for the controlled drilling of deviated (non-vertical) wells with reusable whipstocks, measuring their inclination, and, ultimately, their direction of deviation. (15)

What caused a rebirth of drilling along Huntington Beach's shoreline in the late 1920s and early 1930s? The Newport Inglewood Fault runs along the beach and isolates the Huntington Beach field from the vast deposit of oil under the California Tidelands, just offshore. How to access this bonanza? Drilling off shore was, and remains, very expensive. Directional drilling from onshore was preferable. No offshore drilling platforms, then or now. Apparently, Eastman got the most credit for developing the directional drilling techniques.

Now, with the inventions of Eastman et al, they could drill from onshore locations into the offshore, submerged tidelands. And they did so with a vengeance.

Independent oilmen secretly drilled a number of slanted wells from small town lots east of Ocean Avenue, under the street and through Standard's P. E. Strip where Standard had some 50 producing wells, under the beach and ocean-ward into the tidelands oil pool. In fact, by 1936, nearly 90 wells slanted through the Standard's Strip. But Standard had also drilled (secretly) its own slanted wells into the tidelands field. (16) The new tidelands wells often produced more than 2,000 barrels of oil per day. But questions arose immediately. At least two of Standard's wells in the P. E. Strip lost production because deviated wells had pierced their casings. With 50 wells along the Strip, it was only a matter of time before such an encounter occurred, and Standard was angry. Drilling through Standard's property without permission was an act of criminal trespass, now exacerbated by the piercing.

Even more serious was the fact that the tidelands oil was produced in secret, and incurred NO royalty payments to the city of Huntington Beach, the state of California, or the U. S. Government. That was because title to the tidelands had not been questioned until money became an issue. Then, each governmental entity claimed jurisdiction. That matter occupied lawyers and politicians for several years. The thieves, including Standard Oil, found themselves hauled into court by the State of California, which wanted to be paid. The courts and politicians chose sides among the slant-hole drillers in fights that lasted until title to the tidelands was decided: California out to three nautical miles from shore; the U. S. Government beyond to the international limit of three leagues (about 10 miles.) Controversy continues to simmer over details of title, but the three-mile limit for the state remains. (17)

This story is about Texas oil and oilmen, not California; but the stories are parallel. For the long story of the fights among California politicians, independent oilmen, Standard Oil of California, and the federal government regarding stolen oil from the California Tidelands, see the books by Bartley and by Sabin, Notes 4 and 9.

NOTES

1. G. R. Hopkins and A. B. Coons, 1934, "Crude petroleum and petroleum products," in *Statistical Appendix to Minerals Yearbook 1932-33*, US Bureau of Mines, p.306-307; located in Wikipedia 11/30/2018

2. Ann Pepper, *Orange County Register*, p. 23, January 24, 1991; https://www.huntingtonbeachca.gov/files/users/library/complete/090518-22.pdf

3. Barbara Milkovich, *A Brief History of Huntington Beach*, 1986. Quoted in "Huntington Beach's Oil Rush from 1919 to 2010." http://1x57.com/entrepreneurship/huntington-beach-oil-rush-from-1919-to-2010/, accessed November 27, 2018, RC.

4. Delbert G. "Bud" Higgins, "OIL FIELDS A Brief History Of The Oil Fields At Huntington Beach, California," December 1976, pp. 1-5.

5. https://www.huntingtonbeachca.gov/files/users/library/complete/070811-2.pdf, accessed   November 29, 2018, RC.

6. Ernest R. Bartley, *The Tidelands Oil Controversy: A Legal and Historical Analysis*, University of Texas Press, Austin, TX, 1953, p. 70, including footnotes 40 and 41.

7. "Bona Fide Population of Huntington Brach Now Estimated 6,000," *Santa Ana Register*, January 30, 1922, p. 9.

8. Higgins, p. 6. Higgins' table shows production by years and number of wells producing. Unfortunately, he entered the year 1925 twice; but I have chosen to ignore the effects of the double entry. Perhaps, the second 1925 entry should be for 1926, and the subsequent entries adjusted accordingly. The effect remains inconsequential nearly 100 years later. .

9. "Save Thousands After Test at Garden Grove," *Santa Ana Register*, February 23, 1922, p. 6.

10. Paul Sabin, "Beaches Versus Oil" in *Land of Sunshine*, William Deverell and Greg Hise, eds., University of Pittsburgh Press, Pittsburgh, PA, 2005. P. 104.

11. Paul Sabin, *Crude Politics: The California Oil Market 1900-1940*, University of California Press, Berkeley, CA, 2005.

12. Thomas E. Stimson, Jr., "Oil Drillers Throw Curves," in *Popular Mechanics*, January 1950, pp. 161 – 164; 250, & 252.

13. Sterling Gleason, "Slanted Oil Wells Work New Marvels," in *Popular Science Monthly*, May 1934, pp. 40. 41, 117.

14. Higgins; See Note 4.

15. Robert Farrar, "Huntington Beach, A Portrait in Oil and Water," *Orange County Illustrated*, April 1967, pp. 31, 32,https://huntingtonbeachca.gov/files/users/library/complete/070920-3.pdf, accessed 12/10/2018. RC.

16. "State Oil Probers Make Plans for Survey of H. B. Field; First Meeting Held," *Santa Ana Register*, August 29, 1935, p.1.

17. A whipstock is a steel wedge that can be inserted in the drill hole at a predetermined angle. The drill bit glances off the whipstock and the drill string goes forward at the chosen angle. The Eastman removable whipstock can be taken from its original position and, after inclination and directional measurements, replaced deeper in the (now deviated) hole. The process is repeated until the bit arrives at the target in the oil-bearing stratum. This was the technology of the day. Horizontal drilling, developed mainly by George Mitchell for drilling into the Barnett Shale near Fort Worth, has made whipstocking obsolete.

18. R. W. Jimerson, "Tidelands Wells May Boost Yield," *San Francisco Examiner*, October 21, 1936, Main Edition, p. 20.

19. The U. S. Supreme Court decided in 1947 that the tidelands belonged to the United States rather than to the coastal states. But Eisenhower's campaign promise to support legislation to reverse the Court's decision garnered him the votes of coastal states, especially California and Texas. Congress passed the Submerged Lands Act that gave California title to its tidelands to three nautical miles seaward, and to Texas, three leagues seaward. Arguments over some details continue to this day. https://nauticalcharts.noaa.gov/publications/docs/shore-and-sea-boundaries/volume-3/cse-library-shalowitz-p1.pdf; "The Tidelands Litigation" See p. 142; (no author listed).

CHAPTER 6
REGULATION IN EAST TEXAS

Between the Spindletop and East Texas discoveries, the Texas Railroad Commission tried to establish rules, primarily, spacing among wells and production allowables, but both the majors and independents challenged the legality of the proposed rules and delayed any real regulation of the oil field activities. The commission had a meager budget and it effectively allowed oil and gas interests to regulate themselves in those early days.

Then, in 1932, Governor Ross Sterling appointed Col. Ernest O. Thompson to fill a vacancy on the three-person commission. At last, the commission had a strong and impartial leader. (1)

Ernest Thompson was an entrepreneur at an early age. As an 11-year-old boy in 1903, he delivered newspapers throughout all of Amarillo, which at the time had only 1,500 inhabitants. By the time he had graduated from high school in 1910, he had amassed a small fortune of $2,000 and owned a drug store that he bought with his paperboy money.

Thompson spent his freshman year of college in 1910 at Virginia Military Institute (VMI) because he liked military matters. But an epidemic of conjunctivitis forced VMI to close in the spring. Thompson spent the rest of the year at Eastman Business College in Poughkeepsie, New York, where he learned shorthand. After that, he worked for a year selling Willys Overland cars (he sold more than 2,000) before enrolling in the University of Texas in the fall of 1912.

Shortly after his arrival in Austin, he met Judge Reuben Gaines, a former Chief Justice of the Texas Supreme Court. The judge hired Thompson to be his chauffeur and private secretary, with all expenses paid—a room at the Driskill Hotel (where the Gaineses lived), meals, and laundry plus a salary of $50 per month. Gaines taught his young protégé much about the law and people, and especially how to make meticulously detailed plans for the future. Ernest had accompanied Judge and Mrs. Gaines in Europe when World War I erupted in the summer of 1914. (2)

The threesome returned to America in September, and shortly thereafter Judge Gaines died in Thompson's arms on October 13, 1914, following a stroke. Mrs. Gaines persuaded Thompson to continue living in the Driskill and to continue working for her while he went to college. Ernest graduated and began law school in Austin, but upon the American declaration of war in April 1917, he, the class president, and all but two people in his class joined the U.S. Army. In June, the law school delivered their diplomas to the class at the officers' training camp at Leon Springs, just west of San Antonio.

Ernest joined the U.S. Expeditionary Forces and went to France. There, as a captain, he commanded the 344th Machine Gun Battalion and was promoted to major in 1918. In the war's last battle, Meuse-Argonne, Thompson instructed his men to establish three machine gun battalions behind the advancing infantry, with French 75mm cannons behind the machine guns and 155mm howitzers behind the 75's. The infantry and machine guns marched forward toward the Germans on November 2, 1918, with a deadly canopy of bullets and shells to cover the American advance that settled the outcome. For his leadership, Thompson won a battlefield promotion to lieutenant colonel.

He remained in Europe as part of the occupation force and then returned to Amarillo in 1919. There he became a real estate magnate and married Metropolitan Opera star May Peterson in 1923. He was elected mayor in 1928 and served until June 4, 1932, when former Governor (1921–1925) Pat Neff resigned from the Railroad Commission to become president of Baylor University. Governor Sterling appointed Thompson to Neff's vacated seat.

Thompson quickly became the dominant commissioner, due to the strength of his personality, his clear thinking, and his complete lack of allegiance to any faction. He went to East Texas in 1933 and personally confronted the hot oil dealers and others who were flouting Texas laws. The hot oil dealers were selling oil produced illegally in excess of prorated "allowables" during the dark nights. They installed valves that appeared shut when wide open and vice versa. Other misdeeds took place. People blew up pipelines to protest proration.

East Texas was a rough place in the early days of the oil boom. And in that environment of profligacy, Ernest Thompson became famous as the "Father of Petroleum Conservation." Because he was concerned with protecting the state's natural resources, he often clashed with other commissioners who were more interested in the protection of their independent operator friends than the fate of their state's natural resources.

The Texas Legislature adopted the Rule of Capture, originally from English common law, as law in 1904. Simply put, if I produce oil or gas by means of a legal well sited on my tract of land, and the oil or gas originally under your tract of land flows into my well, that oil in my well is my oil, not yours. You could have recovered it yourself with your own well had you been willing and able. This rule encouraged early drillers in Texas to drill wells as rapidly as possible and as densely as possible. It resulted in overproduction and waste that led to unnecessarily rapid movement of water into the field from the west, especially in the Kilgore area.

The commission adopted a new spacing rule, Rule 37, in the early 1930s that limited drilling to one well per 10 acres. But owners of smaller tracts got their exceptions that led to the drilling of a few hundred wells on leases as small as a half-acre, as well as to a few occasions where wells physically abutted others.

By the mid-1930s, the flagrant over-drilling problems that were generated by application of the Rule of Capture and exceptions to Rule 37 had been resolved in part by the governor's sending the National Guard to the oil field and by legal action. But "by 1935, 29 major companies owned 10,410 wells in the reservoir, and more than a thousand small firms owned over 12,000 wells." (3) The larger operators attempted to limit the rates of production and the density of wells drilled in East Texas by regulatory action, but the small operators and landowners had greater clout with the commission. Reasonable demands for regulation failed in both the Legislature and the commission. The commission set allowables on a per-well basis rather than per acre, and the Legislature refused to institute mandatory pooling. By 1940, the spacing of wells in the East Texas Oil Field settled at one well per five acres, with numerous exceptions for smaller tracts.

Engineering studies sponsored by Big Oil indicated that by 1940, 6,500 wells strategically located on 20-acre spacing could drain the 140,000-acre field more efficiently than could the 25,921 producing wells extant on January 1, 1941. But exceptions to the commission's spacing rules had already allowed 874 wells drilled on leases of less than one acre and a total of 2,100 wells on leases smaller than two acres. (4)

The Legislature met in April 1931, just seven months after the discovery of the Black Giant when the Daisy Bradford #3 blew in, and passed three bills that became law and were important to oil drilling and production in the state.

The first, House Bill 19, prohibited the transport of crude oil or petroleum in Texas that was produced from illegally-drilled wells.

The second, Senate Bill 337, The Marginal Well Act, defined a marginal well in the East Texas Oil Field as one incapable of producing 20 barrels of oil per day. The Act provided that proratable wells, those capable of producing at least 20 barrels per day, were restricted by the commission to producing no more than that amount for a set number of days per month, depending on demand. Marginal wells were allowed to produce at capacity every day.

By 1932, the small operators had figured out that the proration (limitation) of production was in their best interest. They finally supported the commission's authority to set production allowables, largely due to the political skill of the new commissioner, Col. Thompson.

Then, on November 12, the Legislature passed the third law, the Market Demand Act, and adjourned. Governor Ross Sterling signed it quickly. It allowed the commission to set production allowables at market demand. The idea was to balance supply and demand. Some free-marketers would cringe today.

The commissioners have rarely been a cohesive bunch. Thompson and Charles Terrell (appointed to the commission in August 1924) always outvoted Lon Smith, but Jerry Sadler was elected and replaced Terrell in January 1939. Now, Sadler, who disliked Thompson, and Smith routinely outvoted Thompson. Then, Olin Culberson, an outspoken supporter of the independents, was elected to the commission and was seated in January 1941, replacing Smith. Thompson was able to maintain his reputation as independent of political influence because he was independently wealthy from his own real estate ventures and he owned no interests or stock in any oil ventures. His interests were to get maximum benefit for Texas and Texans from the Black Giant. Only after the commissioners whose parochial interests meant they always favored the independent operators against the major companies departed the commission—that is, only after Sadler, Smith, and Culberson were gone—could Thompson lead the commission to become primarily dedicated to the preservation of the resources of the state.

Beauford Jester defeated and replaced Sadler in 1942 and remained a commissioner until he was elected governor in 1947. Upon his being seated as governor, Jester appointed William J. Murray Jr. as his successor on the commission. Jester died in July 1949, whereupon Lt. Governor Allan Shivers assumed the governorship. In general, the commissioners strove to keep the wealth and jobs derived from Texas oil within Texas and among Texans. The integrated oil companies just had to deal with this prejudice.

The commission attempted to improve management oil resources by changing the rules again in 1957. The average acreage per well had been about four acres between 1940 and 1957, so it was easy to adopt a new rule requiring a spacing of five acres per well. But old wells were exempted from this new rule. In 2019, the minimum acreage assignable to a new well in the East Texas Oil Field remains five acres, but no new wells are being drilled because the field is mostly depleted, and the remaining wells produce too much salt water to be very profitable.

By 1960, market demand was low enough, in part due to the importation of foreign oil, for the commission to curtail production to eight days per month for proratable wells. Marginal wells were exempt from this restriction. The result was that a marginal well producing 15 barrels per day for 30 days per month could produce 450 barrels per month, while a proratable well (one capable of producing more than 20 barrels per day) could only produce 160 barrels (8 x 20) per month. This inequity of the Marginal Well Rule made bribing a poorly-paid state employee for a marginal classification an attractive proposition.

The official rationale for adopting the Marginal Well Rule was that marginal wells that could only produce small amounts of oil might be damaged if they were to be turned off and on at frequent intervals. By allowing them to produce continually, the lives of these wells could be extended. In fact, the rule was an invitation for bribery.

In order to appreciate the effects of the Marginal Well Rule's limitation on the oil production from proratable wells, consider an 20-acre lease with one well (legal or illegal) capable of producing 60 barrels per day. It would be restricted to 160 barrels per month. But if it were classified as a marginal well, it could be connected to three dummy wells (five acres each), and the 60 barrels could be made to appear spread evenly among the four at 15 barrels per day. Thus the lease could produce from one actual well 450 barrels per month for an extra 290 illegal barrels.

No law or rule prohibiting the drilling of non-vertical wells existed until the commission adopted Rule 54 in April 1949. It stated, "... no well shall be intentionally deviated without permission from the commission." Of course, the operative word here is "intentionally." The deviators flagrantly dismissed the new rule, forcing the commission to adopt a new rule on May 10, 1961, limiting the maximum deviation of a well to three degrees from the vertical and requiring an inclination measurement at every 500 feet of depth.

The commission's ill-defined rules and loose enforcement of those rules left the Texas oil fields ripe for abuse. When the majors or independents were reprimanded for being on the wrong side of a rule, they defended themselves vigorously, thereby entangling the commission in hearings and litigation that required time and money. Conditions for the perfect storm—the inevitable slant-hole affair in the oil field—included the long-held animus of many East Texans toward Big Oil, geology, and politics.

NOTES

1. James A. Clark, *Three Stars for the Colonel: The Biography of Ernest O. Thompson, Father of Petroleum Conservation*, Random House, New York, NY, 1954.

2. *Handbook of Texas Online*, Randolph B. Campbell, "GAINES, REUBEN REID," accessed December 29, 2018, http://www.tshaonline.org/handbook/online/articles/fga06.

3. David F. Prindle, *Petroleum Politics and the Texas Railroad Commission*, University of Texas Press, Austin, TX, 1981, p. 49.

4. East Texas Engineering Association, *The East Texas Oil Field 1930–1940*, privately printed, pp. 22-24. A CD of *The East Texas Oil Field 1930–1950* is available from the East Texas Geological Society, 102 North College Avenue, Suite 1200, Tyler, TX 75702.

CHAPTER 7
THE FIRST DEVIATED WELLS IN EAST TEXAS

By the close of 1945, the East Texas field had produced about a third of the original oil in place—2.26 billion barrels. That's oil on which severance tax had been paid to the state. Nobody knows how much additional hot oil had been produced through the 23,507 wells that were still producing at the time. (1) The column of salty water that drives the oil into the geologic trap (and into the oil wells) moves into the space formerly occupied by the produced oil, and the oil-water contact moves upward and eastward. Thus, wells that produced from the western side of the field ultimately produced mostly, or only, salty water.

Robert Allgood was six years old when he moved from Dallas to Longview in 1946 with his mother and father, Sadie and Reid Allgood. I knew of Robert through my parents, whose friendship with the Allgoods was tight, but I had no substantive interaction with him until 2006. That's when I called the Goody Goody wine store in Dallas where, unknown to me, Robert worked. I called about picking up wine I had ordered a week earlier. (2)

Robert answered my call, "Goody Goody. This is Robert."

"Robert, this is Bob Cargill."

"You're not Bob Cargill. I knew Bob Cargill, and he's dead."

"I'm his son. I'll be at your shop shortly to collect the wine I ordered last week. I look forward to meeting you."

I collected my wine and talked with Robert about the slant-hole days in East Texas for about 10 minutes. Robert explained that in response to the call for a whipstocker, the Allgoods moved to Longview.

Reid Allgood had been an employee of John Eastman's oil well surveying company and was living in Dallas in 1946. He had worked in and around the East Texas Oil Field since 1932 and was an expert whipstocker. He knew just how to direct the drill bit in the desired direction by placing a whipstock in the hole being drilled so that the bit would glance off at the desired angle and direction. He could guide the drill bit very near any desired location up to a mile away. (3)

By 1946, wells on the western side of the field had begun to produce salt water. The major companies that owned some of these wells asked the Eastman Company to send an expert whipstocker to East Texas who would to drill deviated wells eastward into the remaining oil. These deviated wells would replace their "watered-out" wells. Reid Allgood was the man. (4)

Allgood drilled an unknown number of deviated wells for the major companies. But without the records of these wells, there is no way of knowing whether they illegally crossed lease lines. After drilling these wells for the majors, Allgood then realized he could apply the same technique for his own benefit.

In that first conversation, Robert told me that his father had met and formed a cabal with Harry Harrington, John Baton, and Ralph Massad. I had heard of these men, but knew only Harrington. He was a short, balding, and aggressively arrogant man. He was bright and thought he was the smartest man in town. An Eagle Scout, Harry was ubiquitous in Boy Scout circles, but most of his contemporaries in Longview regarded him as an insufferable blowhard. Janie Baton Finney, told me during an interview in her home in Kilgore in July 2013 about her father. John Baton had pumped wells for R. E. Smith, a big-time Texas oilman, including two of Smith's wells on the "World's Richest Acre" in downtown Kilgore. He had a fifth-grade education, but he was an expert at just about any oil field job. Operators relied upon Baton for work well done. The cabal agreed that Harrington, the lawyer, would do all the legal work and that the others would handle financing, lease acquisition, and drilling. Allgood would provide the drilling and deviation expertise. Massad seems to have avoided the publicity that Harrington attracted. I found that he was indicted in Wood County, but very little else of interest.

The cabal drilled deviated wells from east of the Woodbine pinchout back westerly into the oil-bearing sand, knowing this was illegal when they started. Drilling permits, which required some credible reason to believe oil was directly below the proposed drill site, for these east-side wells were easy to get (by bribes, if necessary), but earlier dry holes had shown the general location of the Woodbine pinchout.

M. X. "Zerky" Hobbs, Sadie Allgood's brother-in-law, was another expert whipstocker. By 1947, the Allgood group began to buy leases known to be east of the Woodbine pinchout. They drilled on these leases, whipstocking the bit westerly and into the Woodbine Sand. Because the drilling crews and the suppliers of pipe and other equipment had to know what was happening, Allgood and others paid these accomplices to keep quiet. He paid Zerky $600 per well to do the whipstocking, thereby keeping himself physically out of the operations.

The cabal was not alone in the drilling of deviated wells in the 1940s. I have personal knowledge of some of those early wells because I was present in January 1949 when, with great ceremony, one of them, John Wrather's W. L. Bussey well, was dedicated to the Boy Scouts. (Title to the well was publicly handed to the Boy Scouts and Girl Scouts.)

The Railroad Commission had recognized that slant-hole drilling had been a potential problem in 1950. That's when Ed Stanley, then an engineer working for the commission, wrote a letter to the commission on April 19. He questioned inclination surveys filed with the commission, noting that he had received evidence of deviated wells completed as producing wells in areas that had already been proved barren. (5) His letter gave specific recommendations for controlling slant-hole drilling. And on May 2, 1950, commissioners Murray and Thompson issued a memo to operators containing Stanley's recommendations. Operators and commission personnel often honored these recommended procedures.

The Railroad Commissioners in 1961 were Thompson (from 1932), Olin Culberson (from 1941), and William J. Murray Jr. (from 1948). The commission suffered from the severe illnesses of both Col. Thompson and Olin Culberson in 1961. Culberson died that same year and was replaced in September by former Lt. Governor Ben Ramsey. Thompson, though incapacitated, held office until January 1965. Ramsey's inexperience as a regulator left him ineffective. Murray, serving as chairman between 1961 and 1963, was essentially alone in handling the scandal that was about to erupt.

Bill Murray began his public career as a senior petroleum engineer at the commission in 1939 and there established his reputation as a conservationist. He worked to conserve the oil that drove the Texas economy, and he fought to end the practice of flaring natural gas that was produced along with crude oil.

A native of Coleman, Texas, Murray grew up in the oil fields of West Texas, where his father was an independent oil operator and a part owner of Brannon Oil and Gas Company in Abilene. He was an Eagle Scout and an outstanding student at the University of Texas, where he earned both a bachelor's and a master's degree in petroleum engineering in 1936 and 1938, respectively. A Boy Scout scholarship financed his education at UT in part. He remained at the university briefly to teach and do research before joining his father at Brannon as engineer, geologist, and lease superintendent. (6)(7)

NOTES

1. James S. Hudnall, "East Texas Field," *Occurrence Of Oil And Gas In Northeast Texas*, Frank A. Herald, Ed., University of Texas Publication No. 5116: August 15, 1951, Austin, TX, pp. 113-118.

2. I had two conversations with Robert Allgood, the first, on August 26, and the second, on December 13, 2006, both at the Goody Goody Liquor in Dallas. Alas, I did not record those discussions, but I did write notes immediately afterward. Robert's remarks made lasting impressions on me. I met Robert again on August 11, 2010, when I showed him a draft of the chapter in which I repeated what he had told me in our interviews. That was for an early version of this book. When he realized that I was including the names of the people involved, he became upset, stating that grandchildren of the deviators should not learn of their granddaddy's fallibility. I left. We have not spoken since.

3. My use of the term "directional drilling" implies legal non-vertical wells drilled within a lease. "Slant-hole drilling" and "deviated wells" imply illegal directional drilling beyond one's lease into that of another.

4. Although the drilling of slanted wells at Huntington Beach had been widely reported in the California press, I have found not one person involved in the similar activity in Texas who was aware of it. And, yes, it did appear in Texas' major newspaper: (a) "Tideland Survey To Protect State Oil Is Planned," *Dallas Morning News*, January 4, 1936; (b) "How to Get All

Energy From Gas Talked at A. P. I.," *The Dallas Morning News*, June 4, 1937, p. 8.; and "Oil! Texas' No. 1 Industry Taps Vaster Resources By Directional Drilling," *The Dallas Morning News*, January 14, 1940, p.1, Rotogravure picture section, with drawings and photos furnished by the Eastman Oil Well Survey Company.

5.   In oil field jargon, after a well has been drilled to the target stratum, several further operations are necessary—logging to determine whether the well might be a producer; setting two strings of pipe (tubing and casing); cementing the casing in the hole; perforating the casing; setting production valves (the Christmas Tree); and others. The "completion" of a well comprises these tasks.

6.   James A. Clark and Michael T. Halbouty, *The Last Boom*, Random House, New York, NY, 1972, p. 277. Ed Stanley was the son of Captain E. N. Stanley, who had been Col. Thompson's enforcer in the early days of the East Texas boom.

7.   http://www.cemetery.state.tx.us/pub/user_form.asp?pers_id=8520.

CHAPTER 8
MURRAY TO THE RAILROAD COMMISSION

The flames of burning gas lit the East Texas skies at night until 1947. In the late 1930s and early 40s, I often stood in my grandfather's yard mesmerized by the orange flames shooting skyward from the wells on his farm. In the early days of the East Texas field, the capture and transport of natural gas was uneconomical, and the producers burned (flared) the produced gas. Murray considered flaring to be a waste of a valuable resource. His expertise took him to Washington, DC, in 1941 to work with the government's Petroleum Administration for War and its predecessor, the Office of Petroleum Coordination, where he was responsible for making sure that oil needed by the Allied Forces was available. (1) Col. Thompson had urged the federal government to authorize what became the Big Inch Pipeline from Longview, Texas, to Phoenixville, Pennsylvania.

Thompson wasn't the only one who pressed for a pipeline to deliver Texas oil to East Coast refineries, however. Secretary of the Interior Harold Ickes and officers of Big Oil also recommended to President Roosevelt the construction of such a pipeline to avoid exposing oil tankers to German submarines. Built during 1942 and 1943, the pipeline carried 300,000 barrels of East Texas oil per day to East Coast refineries for the war effort. The construction of the Big Inch and Little Big Inch pipelines is an inspiring story of government and industry cooperation. General George C. Marshall later said, "No plane failed to fly, no ship failed to sail, and no truck was ever delayed for want of oil." (2)

Murray learned during his tenure in Washington that the Railroad Commission carried considerable influence regarding oil and gas well beyond the borders of Texas. After the war, he returned to Austin to work at the commission. The commission quickly named him chairman of its Gas Conservation Engineering Committee. In this capacity, Murray pushed hard to stop the flaring of natural gas and attracted the attention of Beauford Jester, then a Railroad Commissioner and a candidate for governor. Jester had served in the Meuse-Argonne at the same time as Col. Thompson and was a victim of poison gas. As newly-elected governor in 1947, Jester appointed Murray to the commission seat he had just vacated. (3) As a member of the commission, Murray gained the political clout that he needed to stop the flaring of gas. The commission ordered all the oil fields in Texas shut down until facilities for recovery and treatment of the produced gas could be installed. In forcing the recovery of produced natural gas the commission virtually created the worldwide natural gas industry. (4) Once the gas was recovered, it became a cheap commodity to be used as fuel and as feedstock for the petrochemical industry. (5)

That Murray owned a part interest in his father's Brannon Oil and Gas Company was a matter of public knowledge when Jester appointed him to the Railroad Commission; in fact, his experience with Brannon was among the list of qualifications for the appointment. For once, the commission could have one commissioner who was competent to understand the industry he would regulate. Nor was Murray a political climber as have been nearly all other commissioners before and since Murray. He was an engineer who saw problems and tried to go about solving them rationally. Alas, he had few political skills. (6)

NOTES

1. Petroleum Administration for War, author, *Petroleum Administration for War*, 1941–1945, John W. Frey, and H. Chandler Ide, Eds. University Press of the Pacific, Honolulu, HI, 2005.

2. "The Big Inch and Little Big Inch Pipelines, the Most Amazing Government-Industry Cooperation Ever Achieved," The Louis Berger Group, Inc., 120 Halsted Street, East Orange, NJ 07019. See http://historicmonroe.org/labor/pix/inchlines.pdf.

3. My great-uncle, Martin Hays, mentioned earlier, took me to meet Governor Jester in his office in 1948. Tall cotton for a 13-year-old boy.

4. David F. Prindle, *Petroleum Politics and the Texas Railroad Commission*, Austin, TX, 1981, pp. 41-69.

5. I met Murray in the early 1980s when I joined my father at meetings of the Texas Independent Producers & Royalty Owners Association (TIPRO).

6. I became acquainted with most of the commissioners in office between 1980 and 2000, and I watched the commission's activities. My statements here are based on those observations.

After the cabal had begun drilling deviated wells, it wasn't long before others decided they, too, could find easy profit via their own deviated wells. Thus John E. Wrather, a highly-respected East Texas oilman, began acquiring leases along the eastern edge of the East Texas field in 1946, and, presumably, outside the field's eastern limit. Thus he bought the W. L. Bussey (49.4 acres), the adjacent (west and south, respectively) J. H. Alexander (50 acres), and M. E. Alexander (14 acres) leases. Wrather drilled seven wells on the Bussey lease between May 29, 1946, and July 2, 1948. Likewise, he drilled 10 wells on the adjacent Alexander lease beginning in December 1946. Each of these wells extended westward into General American's A. H. Tubbs lease and Tidewater's J. Castleberry lease, both immediately west of the Alexander leases. (1) (2)

On October 29, 1948, Wrather assigned a five-acre square in the middle of the Bussey lease to the East Texas Boy Scout Foundation (seven-eighths) and the East Texas Girl Scouts Council (one-eighth). The owners of the mineral estate in the Bussey tract conveyed half of their mineral estate to the Foundation three days later.

The East Texas Boy Scout Foundation had come into being in 1946. A group of East Texas businessmen determined that the East Texas Area Council of the Boy Scouts of America would need a continuing source of funding if it were to operate without fear of the need for annual fund drives. These men created a tax-exempt organization that would support the council's summer camp program from the income earned on donations to the foundation, but in doing so they defied the Boy Scout's National Council, which wanted no local council to have any source of funding that was not subservient to it.

The Railroad Commission granted a permit to Wrather on November 5, 1948, to drill, in the name of the East Texas Boy Scout Foundation,

Inc., a well on the five-acre "Boy Scout" lease, as reported in the Sunday *Houston Chronicle* on November 7, 1948. The well would be known as the East Texas Boy Scout Foundation, Inc.-W. L. Bussey #1. The *Houston Chronicle* quoted the commission as saying it believed this was the first known instance of the Boy Scouts or any similar organization's drilling its own well. In applying to the commission for the permit to drill, Wrather told the commission, "It is anticipated that the drilling of this well can be financed in Gregg County by the citizens, independent oil operators, and oil companies and others wishing to participate." He also stated, "Funds from the foundation will be used to create additional facilities for Scouting and also to provide funds in the future if economic conditions make it impossible to maintain the regular financing program of Scouting in the East Texas area."

Who was John E. Wrather?

I never met Mr. Wrather, who lived on my street in Longview, but I knew his older son, John McDonald, who coached us little boys on the vacant lot near the Wrather home. John M., as we called him, died in 1979, and a second son, John David, considerably younger than I, now operates the remaining oil business begun by his father. I know John David, who unfortunately disposed of all his father's old records, leaving nothing for me to examine for this book.

John E. Wrather's father, John Devereaux Wrather, owned the Overton Refinery Company that was sited within the oil field near the town of Overton. Both of John Devereaux Wrather's sons, John Devereaux Jr. (Jack) and John Elgin (John E.), by different wives, worked at their father's refinery as young men. John E. had two sons, John M. and John David, by different wives. John E.'s half-brother Jack married the daughter of Governor W. Lee "Pappy" O'Daniel. Jack's second marriage was to movie star Bonita Granville. Jack created a multimillion-dollar fortune in oil, movies, television, radio, and hotel resorts, and he served in Ronald Reagan's "Kitchen Cabinet." In 1940, John E. left the Overton Refinery to form Waverly & Wrather Drilling Contractors with his friend Fred Waverly in Kilgore. He brought King Cline, who had worked at the refinery, along as accountant and office manager. (3)

With the outbreak of World War II, the U.S. Coast Guard Reserve conscripted boats and yachts of some private citizens to patrol the Gulf Coast for German submarines. John E. owned a cabin cruiser anchored at Galveston and volunteered his boat, himself, and King Cline as temporary Coast Guard reservists. Wrather's friend and attorney, Fred Erisman, occasionally joined Wrather and Cline on patrol.

On the crisp afternoon of Friday, January 14, 1949, John E. Wrather dedicated the Bussey #1 well to the East Texas Boy Scout Foundation and the East Texas Girl Scout Council. The dedication included the blessings of the Texas Railroad Commission and Humble Oil Company. Scouts from Troop 201, my troop, were there as color guard, and I, a 14-year-old sophomore at Longview High School, participated. Wrather (the actual operator) and his partners were present for the ceremony. Harry Harrington, Eagle Scout and operator of a nearby (deviated) lease, acted as master of ceremonies.

This dedication celebrated a great philanthropic event in East Texas of which the Boy Scouts of the East Texas Area Council (ETAC) were the prime benefactors. In fact, with this source of income to the Boy Scouts and the beneficence of several other well-to-do East Texans, the ETAC became the envy of all Scouting.

The event that Friday afternoon attracted approximately 200 friends and neighbors who heard Harrington introduce Wrather and his partners as the generous donors of the well.

Mayor G. A. McCreight of Longview, another of my neighbors, was present, as were five officials of the Humble Oil & Refining Company, including J. A. Neath, vice president; Harold Potter, division superintendent; R. V. Hanrahan, president of Humble Pipe Line Company; John Bell, division petroleum engineer of Humble Oil; and G. A. Lee, district superintendent of the pipeline company. The Humble companies clearly wanted major notice of their participation and support of the project. Leland F. Long and Staley Mims accepted the well from Wrather on behalf of the Boy Scouts and Girl Scouts, respectively.

Several high officials of the state of Texas were also present, including the entire Texas Railroad Commission—Chairman William J. Murray Jr., Col. Ernest O. Thompson, and Olin Culberson—and Secretary of State Paul H. Brown.

Col. Thompson commended the industry for the part it played in securing the well for the Scouts. "It is a gilt-edge investment in the youth of our state." Thompson went on to complain of the importation of foreign oil (even in 1949!) as a threat to the development of domestic reserves and therefore a threat to American domestic security. Thompson said that importation of 500,000 barrels of cheaper foreign oil was already seriously cutting into the demand for domestic oil, which was then selling for about $2.50 per barrel. "We had cut Texas production 250,000 barrels daily in January [1949] allowable because lessened market demand threatened to cause above-ground waste if more oil was produced than required." (4)

Thompson compared the situation to that in the American watchmaking industry. He said that one large company has gone broke and others were threatened as a result of importation of six million watches the previous year, principally from Switzerland. He said the same thing could happen to the petroleum industry.

Olin Culberson, in advising Wrather of the granting of the permit [to drill], wrote, "This is a wonderful thing to do and is another evidence of your big heart."

Chairman Murray, the youngest of the commissioners and the first petroleum engineer to ever serve on that body, wholeheartedly endorsed the action of the men who made this gift possible. He recalled that he owed his higher education to a Boy Scout scholarship.

In an interesting lapse at *TIME*, it reported in its January 24, 1949, issue on page 19, "Texas Oilman Jack Wrather and some of his well-heeled friends decided to make a contribution to the local Boy Scouts; they spent $22,000 in drilling a well near Longview, struck oil, turned the operation over to the boys. Expected income: $900 a month, plus $125 for Girl Scouts." *TIME* should have named John E. Wrather, not his half-brother Jack, who had nothing to do with the Boy Scout well or the slant-hole matter.

NOTES

1. The eastern edge of the Woodbine sand is not a "knife edge" with a single sharp pinchout. Rather there are as many as five fingers with the top-most finger extending eastward the least, and the lower fingers extending farther eastward. At their extremities, the fingers may be separated by several feet. When drilling "straight" wells, many drillers who did not encounter the Woodbine at the expected uppermost depth, considered the well a dry hole. Because of this lack of geological sophistication, they failed to drill deeper to find the unexpected fingers, and unnecessarily abandoned wells that would have produced plenty of oil. My father drilled his T. B. Harris 2-A well in which he barely touched the eastern edge of the uppermost of the Woodbine fingers. From what he interpreted to be one inch of Woodbine thickness, he produced about four barrels of oil per day for more than 18 years. Then, in the early 1990s, I acquired the remaining interest in the old well and agreed with a second operator, who had considerable geological expertise, to redrill the well up to 15 feet deeper in the same borehole. Within a few days, the redrilled well, penetrating a deeper and more eastward finger of the Woodbine, produced 18 barrels of oil per day for several years.

2. Oil leases are generally referred to as follows: Operator's name, followed by surface owner's name. Thus, The General American A. H. Tubbs lease; or Tidewater's J. Castleberry lease.

3. Cline, Jerry K., *Born and Raised: An American Story of Adoption*, Xlibris Corporation, Bloomington, IN, 2010. Jerry is the adopted son of King Cline.

4. *Longview Daily News*, January 14, 1949; Robert M. Hayes, "East Texas Scout Group Becomes Oil Well Owner," *The Dallas Morning News*, January 15, 1949, p. 7; *Fort Worth Star-Telegram*, January 14, 1949, p. 8. Thompson was speaking of the number of barrels of oil allocated to the State of Texas for production in January 1949.

CHAPTER 10
THE QUIET INTERIM

Word of slant-hole drilling circulated among the independent oilmen of East Texas. The active deviators spoke of their exploits only among themselves and with likely joiners. But a permit to drill any well required approval by the Railroad Commission. In East Texas, the commission's Kilgore office approved applications and issued permits for the commission. Ultimately, permits approved in Kilgore usually found approval in Austin.

Among the required information for an application to drill a *straight* well is the exact location and proposed depth of the proposed well, *and* an acceptable argument that the proposed well will be productive.

I raise this matter because most of the deviated wells drilled into the East Texas field were known by commission personnel to lie beyond the presumptive productive limit of the Woodbine sand. That said, the commission regularly granted permits to drill vertical wells (that turned out to have been deviated) that—had they been straight—would have missed the Woodbine according to the commission's maps. The commission engineers who approved the bogus permits needed protection and/or bribes from their beneficiaries.

By 1950, slant-hole drilling had become sufficiently common that Edwin G. Stanley, a respected engineer in the commission's Kilgore office, wrote a letter to Commission Chair Bill Murray on April 1, 1949:

> *Dear Sir:*
>
> *As discussed with you during your recent visit to this office, there is a dire need for additional restrictions for drilling of wells in the East Texas field. This office has received various rumors as to the drilling of directionally deviated wells. Although none have been substantiated, there are certain indications there have been and will be wells directionally drilled in areas previously proven dry and completed as producing wells.* " (1), (2)

Clark and Halbouty continue to quote from Stanley's letter where he questioned the "accuracy of the inclination surveys filed with the Commission," indicating that no one really knew where the well might be bottomed. Stanley further provided suggestions for eliminating, or, at least, reducing, slant-hole drilling. Commissioners Murray and Thompson sent Stanley's recommendations "almost verbatim" to all operators in the field on May 2, 1950, a testament to the esteem with which Stanley was held by his superiors.

From outward appearances, the matter of deviated wells in East Texas remained quiet from 1950 until 1960. At least, the commission took no action seen by the public. But Humble Oil, perhaps others, took advantage of a little-known program approved by the Department of Public Safety. The DPS permitted large companies with many employees —railroads and major oil producers—which experienced much internal theft, to appoint "Special Rangers,"which were *not* connected in any way with the real Texas Rangers.

My late friend, retired Texas Ranger Glenn Elliott, explained to me in one of our dozens of long visits before his death on December 31, 2012, that the number of Texas Rangers had always been small (there were only 62 in 1962). Investigations of large numbers of apparent crimes, especially involving oil companies and railroads, would overwhelm the Texas Rangers' manpower. Thus, some investigators for oil companies and railroads were given Special Ranger status. These Special Rangers had authority to carry weapons but could not make arrests. They were paid by their employers and not by the state of Texas.

From the late 1950s, Humble Oil, and perhaps other companies, sent their Special Rangers to East Texas to seek information about who might be involved in theft from Humble via deviated wells.

NOTES

1. Edwin G. Stanley was the son of Capt. E. N. Stanley, Col. Garrison's trusted assistant. My impression, gleaned from conversations with some of the few remaining old oilfield hands, is that the younger Stanley was always eager to help young beginning oilmen with technical problems. For that he was well liked. See Clark and Halbouty, *The Last Boom*, p. 277 for a more detailed version of this vignette.

2. HGIC Report, p.11. The remainder of Stanley's letter is not available.

CHAPTER 11
THE LAWYERS

Personal relationships remain among the most important factors in determining the fates of individuals and organizations. Interference with such relationships can lead to unpleasant consequences. Take the case of John E. Wrather and his close friend and personal attorney, Fred R. Erisman Jr.

Wrather, mentioned earlier in Chapter 9, had already drilled more than 18 deviated oil wells in the 1940s, and he must have assumed that his theft would eventually be found out. He would need the best defense counsel available. That would be Fred Erisman. The two men had formed a close relationship in the 1940s when their offices were next door in the old First National Bank building in downtown Longview. Erisman had been one of the dignitaries at the dedication of Wrather's Boy Scout well in January 1949. I don't know whether he knew at the time that the well was deviated.

Erisman was diagnosed with cancer in 1950 and Wrather arranged for his admission to the Mayo Clinic in Minnesota. There, Erisman's doctors told him his cancer was terminal and that he had about six months to live. Erisman quickly went to the newly opened M. D. Anderson Clinic in Houston where new experimental treatments gave him a new lease on life. He lived very well for another 28 years during which time he felt an obligation to Wrather beyond that of friend and colleague.

I am sure, without definitive evidence, that Wrather must have explained his potential liability in the slant-hole matter to Erisman, and that the latter knew he would sooner or later be called upon to defend his friend when the inevitable collapse of the illegal enterprise came.

Erisman, a native of Fort Worth and an honor graduate of Texas Christian University in 1929, never attended law school but gained admission to the bar in 1931. He came to Longview shortly thereafter to take advantage of the opportunities presented by the new oil boom.

He was a scholar of the law. He studied every aspect of cases in which the law is complex and often misread, even by lawyers. He devoured the weekly advance sheets that contained recently decided opinions of appellate courts. He also prepared indexed lists of all reversals according to the issues involved. At trial, he argued each case from an outline of questions he prepared for the kind of case being tried based on his reading of the advance sheets. Governor Allan Shivers appointed Erisman judge of the 124th Judicial District of Gregg County in 1950. He served there until he retired to private practice of law in 1955. He combined his notes into his respected book *Reversible Errors in Texas Criminal Cases* published in 1956. Criminal defense attorneys Arch C. McColl III and S. Michael McColloch revised that text, and today it's in its third edition under the title *Erisman's Reversible Errors in Texas Criminal Cases.*

Erisman's connections and intellect, coupled with his broad experience as a trial lawyer and judge, gained him a reputation as a fixer, one whose connections could get almost anything done, and assured his clients that they would get the best legal representation available. (1) Erisman's friend, Tyler lawyer Weldon Holcomb, memorialized him in the magazine of the Texas Criminal Defense Lawyers Association: "Above all other considerations, Judge Erisman was always the epitome of decorum, courtesy and respect, to both the Court and opposing counsel. He was a relentless cross-examiner, and in jury argument he could either be the suave and sophisticated logical counsel with a flair for the grand vocabulary or, if the circumstances required, he could be a "tent revival" chest-thumping, knee-slapping, red-faced evangelist. Regardless of the circumstances, his side of the case was always well represented. As an individual, I am extremely thankful that I had the opportunity to be "educated, chastised, and complimented" by Judge Fred Erisman." (2), (3)

The second primary attorney in the slant-hole matter was Gordon Wellborn of Henderson. Wellborn was born in rural western Rusk County into a large family. He played basketball at Henderson High in the 1920s and won a scholarship to Schreiner Institute (now Schreiner University) before moving on to the University of Texas and UT Law School. He paid his way through the University of Texas as a delivery boy for a local laundry.

After being admitted to the bar, Wellborn returned to Henderson to practice law with his older brother, Harold H. Wellborn (known as H. H.), a veteran of World War I. It wasn't long before the brothers had a falling out from which they never recovered. They hated each other from that day forward. Several observers of the Rusk County Courthouse scene came to watch Gordon and H. H. try cases against each other. Gordon remembered every slight and held intense grudges forever. He was a hard-working lawyer who focused on making money and had little interest in philosophical considerations.

By 1960, Gordon Wellborn was a bitter man. After a brief marriage, he became a confirmed bachelor who hated women. He also hated the government, the Internal Revenue Service, and taxes. He became a political follower of Ronald Reagan. He was paranoid. His office was all white with black furniture and a black-and-red carpet. The office was soundproofed and had no windows, reflecting Wellborn's paranoia. He bought a new white Cadillac with a red interior every year. Wellborn, standing six feet, four inches, and weighing 250 pounds, presented an imposing figure when he approached the jury box. He would lean over into the face of a juror, preferably the foreman, and look him in the eye as if to remind the juror of favors he had done for the family. The tactic usually provided the desired result.

Rex Houston, who joined Wellborn's law firm in 1950, wore expensive tailor-made Oxford suits from Neiman Marcus with coordinating shoes and ties. At six feet and 200 pounds, Houston presented a figure of elegance, and he was a superb trial lawyer. Wellborn's chosen attire was also elegant: Hollywood-brand suits with red silk lining in the jacket, a bold Countess Mara necktie held in place with a stickpin bearing a large diamond, a red silk handkerchief in the breast pocket, and alligator shoes. Houston's forte, personal injury suits, complemented Wellborn's criminal defense expertise. (4)

The social and political climate in East Texas in the 1950s and 1960s, as described earlier, included special animosity toward Big Business that originated outside Texas. The high-powered attorneys from the big cities who represented Big Oil were regarded as carpetbaggers and were at a severe disadvantage in East Texas courts when they opposed Erisman and Wellborn. Even Dallas lawyers who represented major companies got similar treatment. Erisman and Wellborn differed in style, but each in his own way was an effective advocate for his clients.

Erisman and Wellborn represented most of the deviators throughout the slant-hole events of 1962 and 1963.

NOTES

1. My friend and attorney, Glenn Perry, had wanted to join Erisman upon his graduation from the University of Texas Law School, but Erisman wanted no partners. Still, Perry knew a lot about Erisman, and in a discussion of my writing this book on September 26, 2013, Perry told me much about Erisman's approach to the law.

2. Weldon Holcomb, *Voice for the Defense*, June 1978, vol. 7, no. 12, pp. 4–6.

3. The Erismans lived a quarter mile from us on Green Street, and although the Erisman son, Fred III, was a few years younger than I, we knew each other. In fact, the younger Fred entered The Rice Institute (now Rice University) as a freshman in 1954, the year I was a senior. My family held Judge Erisman in the highest regard.

4. Glenn Perry, having failed in his quest to join Erisman's law firm, landed a job with Gordon Wellborn in Henderson. Perry learned much about being a litigator from reading Wellborn's files on the slant-hole matter.

CHAPTER 12
THE END OF A DECADE

As the decade of the 1950s drew inexorably toward its close, the virus that was slant-hole drilling headed toward its eventual explosion. The number of independent oilmen involved in the theft grew rapidly, as did the number of deviated wells being drilled. The thieves continued to expand their exploits while apparently believing they would get away with their deeds.

Between 1953 and 1956, my father Robert Cargill, Ramon Kennimer, and others acquired leases on what became known as the E. E. Stone lease bordering the eastern edge of the Sun Oil T. G. Pressley lease. Kennimer, as operator, employed Gibson Drilling Company to drill the E. E. Stone #1A well after having previously drilled and plugged well #1 as a dry hole. The #1 well was, presumably, a straight well that missed the eastern edge of the Woodbine Sand. The #1A well began to flow oil on November 24, 1956. Kennimer drilled the E. E. Stone #2 well in the summer of 1958, and Cargill took over as operator on August 1, 1960.

Engineers in the commission's Kilgore office classified both Stone wells as "marginal," incapable of producing 20 barrels of oil per day; thus, they were allowed to produce at the level of no more than 20 barrels per day every day after completion. Because Kennimer's records are not available, I don't have the logs, directional surveys, or production data. (1)

This well is of special interest to me because among the mineral owners in the Stone lease are The Rice Institute (aka Rice University) and the Rice family. They collected a share of the royalties produced almost surely without knowledge that the source of their income was a pair of deviated wells. (2)

On the judicial front, former Dallas County District Attorney Will Wilson resigned his seat on the Texas Supreme Court in 1956 to run, successfully, for attorney general.

Wilson had earned a degree in geology at the University of Oklahoma and a law degree at Southern Methodist University. He returned from combat duty in the Philippines after the Japanese surrender in 1945 as a war hero with a Bronze Star.

Wilson was the grandson of a Confederate surgeon and son of a prosperous Dallas businessman. Donald Jackson wrote that Wilson was "aggressive, dynamic, and of unassailable integrity, a winner." (3) He was a popular and successful district attorney from 1946 to 1950 who made sure his attacks on illegal gambling and organized crime were well publicized.

He used his reputation to gain a seat on the Texas Supreme Court in 1950 at age 38, but he was restless there. The *LIFE* article described Wilson as "temperamentally a crime buster, a prosecutor, not a judge." When he resigned from the court to run for attorney general in 1956, Wilson said, according to *LIFE*, "Like the old cavalry general, I've always believed in riding straight for the sound of the guns. Certainly, I know that I am turning my back on the security of a quiet harbor, and certainly the course we steer lies through troubled waters. But that's where the need is greatest."

LIFE quoted an unnamed associate who called Wilson an "unswerving soldier for justice." The associate added, "As attorney general he had the whole state as a stage for his allegorical dramas and he pursued evil wherever he found it." He said further that Wilson routed organized crime in Galveston, pursued the slant-hole drillers in East Texas, the loan sharks, and Billie Sol Estes. His fellow attorneys general elected him as the nation's best in 1960.

My great-grandfather, T. B. Harris, sold a tract of 118 acres on the eastern edge of his considerably larger farm to his daughter (my grandmother) and her husband Bob Wood in 1910 for $10,000. My grandparents farmed this land until Simms Oil Company drilled its Bob Wood #1 well that blew in at 10,000 barrels per day on January 18, 1932, from a depth of 3,540 feet. (4) Income from this and subsequent wells allowed the Woods to pay off the $10,000 although Grandpa Harris had died in late 1931.

Samedan Oil acquired the leasehold and seven producing wells on the farm in January 1942, and drilled an additional three good wells. All 10 producing wells were located in the northwest quadrant of the 118-acre tract. The Railroad Commission at the time did not require the reporting of dry holes drilled, but the eastern edge of the East Texas field was generally defined, and the remainder condemned as barren. My mother told me she saw several dry holes drilled on the remaining acreage where the Woodbine Sand is absent.

Then, in 1960, Samedan sub-leased 55 acres of the eastern part of the farm to a group of Kilgore oilmen operating as Amtex Oil, with Samedan's retaining an overriding royalty interest of 13.75 percent in the farmout. (5), (6) Amtex drilled 11 wells over the next two years, all deviated westerly beyond the western edge of the Wood lease and into the adjoining T. B. Harris lease owned by Continental Oil.

The drilling of deviated wells accelerated in 1960 and well into 1962.

NOTES

1. Civil Action 4171, Sun Oil v. Robert Cargill; Civil Case Files, 1938-, Entry ETX61E, National Archives Identifier 574344; Eastern District of Texas, Tyler Division; RG 21, Records of U.S. District Courts; National Archives at Fort Worth. This and my father's well files provided these facts.

2. The Rice interests came about in 1931 when W. E. Jones and W. R. Hughes conveyed an undivided one-eighth mineral interest in their tract to S. P. Farish, Trustee for the Rice family interests. In 1938, Farish distributed interests to William M. Rice Jr., a nephew of the founder of the institute that bore his name, and his family, as well as to The Rice Institute. I am an active Rice University alumnus and am intrigued by the inclusion of my alma mater as a beneficiary of a slanted well in this story, but I am aware that Rice owns vast mineral interests, as do many other universities.

3. Donald Jackson, *LIFE*, September 21, 1971, pp. 59-62.

4. I have in my files the telegram dated January 19, 1932, in which my grandfather informed my mother, then a freshman at Baylor Belton College, that the Bob Wood #1 had blown in the night before at 10,000 barrels per day.

5. An overriding royalty is an amount deducted from the driller's income and has no effect on the royalty paid to mineral owners. In this case, Samedan would receive 13.75 percent of the gross income derived from all wells drilled by Amtex.

6. The division order dated January 27, 1961, for the Wood lease (copy in my files) shows the division of income from a lease to the various owners.

CHAPTER 13
1961, A BAD YEAR

Although 1960 was relatively calm, 1961 saw heavy activity in the oil patch of East Texas.

Humble Oil owned several leases lying on the eastern edge of the oil field, including the R. E. L. Silvey lease. H. L. "Pete" Long had acquired some leases, including the Mary Smith A, B, and C, just east and southeast of Humble's Silvey lease, and beyond the eastern limit of the field. There he drilled several crooked wells angled back into Humble's Silvey lease. But one day in January 1961, probability caught up with him.

Humble's Silvey #A-22 well began to produce fresh drilling mud. That same day, Long was drilling well #6-A on his Mary Smith lease some 1,300 feet to the southeast. Humble, presumably knowing of the slant-hole activity, concluded that Long's slanted well had accidently pierced its Silvey well. This would explain the appearance of fresh drilling mud in the A-22's oil. With thousands of wells punched into the Woodbine Sand, one for every five acres, sooner or later a slanted well would likely intersect the production pipe of an existing well. Now it had happened.

To make matters worse, Long drilled another slanted well in March 1961, the Mary Smith #1-A, 550 feet south of Humble's Mary Smith #A-2. The #A-2 began to lose production. Fracture stimulation, now called hydraulic fracking, of the Humble well failed, because of a casing leak. Again, Humble suspected that the casing leak resulted from penetration by Long's well. When Humble's engineers discovered drilling mud in the recovered fracture fluid they knew their suspicions were correct. (1), (2)

I met Pete Long shortly after my return to East Texas in 1980. The Longs and Cargills often occupied nearby tables at the Cherokee Club overlooking Lake Cherokee about 10 miles southeast of Longview. Long and my father had been among the group of East Texans who created the Cherokee Water Company and built the lake shortly after World War II. Eventually, they came to a serious disagreement when Long and his followers opposed the construction of a second lake upstream of the present lake, which my father favored. Long and others won the argument, and no second lake ever appeared.

The Pete Long I first met in 1980 was overbearing and not very pleasant, but his wife Virginia was always gracious. I admired her. She was involved in civic affairs and effectively led several local improvement projects. She treated me kindly in all of our meetings. A car wreck nearly ended Pete's life in the mid-1980s, and afterward I found him friendly and eager to please, a changed man in my view. He died in 1989. But in the early 1960s, Pete seemed always ready for a confrontation. He was among the leading drillers of slanted wells, but he got caught in early 1961.

James Wendover, president of Nortex Oil, made a strategic decision. He sold all of Nortex's legitimate production in Louisiana, Oklahoma, and in New Mexico in 1961. He would use the proceeds to buy leases containing 105 wells owned by Ebro Oil on the eastern edge of the East Texas field. Ebro's principal owner and president was W. O. Davis Jr., a 40-year-old graduate of the United States Naval Academy. J. S. Hudnall was a highly respected consulting geologist and partner in Hudnall and Pirtle of Tyler, recognized experts on the East Texas Oil Field. Hudnall evaluated the subject leases for Nortex. He reported that on September 16, 1959, three leases owned by Ebro held future reserves of 4,616,932 barrels of producible oil and future gross revenue of $12,706,357 at $2.75 per barrel. Hudnall never suggested that any of the wells on these leases might be crooked.

Bruce Cunningham, another Naval Academy graduate, was Ebro's vice president. He had banking contacts that helped him engineer loans to Ebro amounting to about $3 million from a collective led by Southwestern Life Insurance Company. Marshall Fagan, head of Southwestern Life's oil loan department, had brought Nortex and Ebro together for the first discussion of a trade in August 1960, and Nortex ultimately agreed to pay $6 million for the leases with Southwestern Life and the banks financing the deal.

Nortex acquired five leases in Rusk County with a total of 46 wells, including the L. R. Jacobs lease. All of these leases sit just east of H.

L. Long's Mary Smith lease, on which Long had drilled several slanted wells. Nortex also bought five more leases comprising 53 acres in Gregg County. Nortex further agreed to absorb Ebro's debt of $1.7 million and to hire Elba Oil Company, another Davis company, to operate the leases until June 1, 1962. The deal closed on February 10, 1961. Shortly thereafter, Davis dissolved Ebro.

Wendover must have been happy with his deal, in which his total cost seems to have been $7.8 million for property allegedly worth nearly $13 million. (3)

Lee Price was a pumper who worked for Shell Oil. His job was to ascertain daily that their well equipment was working properly and that their oil wells were producing at the proper rate. But early on the morning of Wednesday, April 26, 1961, he arrived at Shell's B. F. Laird B #4 well and found fresh drilling mud flowing from a well that had produced clean oil since it was drilled in July 1933, almost 30 years earlier. At 5:30 a.m., Price called Shell's District Superintendent, G. H. Barnes, and asked him to come out to the Laird lease. There, the two men opened the tubing-head valve on the well to find drilling mud surging 30 feet from the wellhead. These experienced field hands recognized that the mud surges matched the strokes of a reciprocating pump used during drilling operations. There was no such pump in sight, so they began to search for one. Before they saw the pump, they heard it. Price and Barnes followed the rhythmic sound and found the culprit on "Bull" Barber's W. B. Goyne #1-A well, located 3,060 feet west-southwest of the Laird B #4. (4), (5) Barber was redrilling his now "watered out" Goyne well in the middle of the oil field where water from the west had invaded. He was deviating his well eastward into the pool of remaining oil, but it accidentally struck Shell's well. The Shell men reported their finding to L. Dwight Murphy, an engineer in the Railroad Commission's Kilgore office. Commission Chairman Bill Murray learned somehow of Barber's deviated well, probably from Murphy, and is alleged to have summoned Barber to Austin where he instructed Barber to repair Shell's well and to cease his illegal activity. Barber returned to Kilgore and accelerated his slant-hole drilling. That's the story as I pieced it together from word I heard on the street.

Humble officers including former Judge Sam Reams met with Federal Petroleum Board officers, including Chairman Dan Purvis, on June 21, 1961, to complain of slant-hole drilling. The Petroleum Board officers told the Humble officers that Humble needed to do its own investigating, but Humble could not require suspected deviators to submit to inspection of their wells. They told the Humble men to take their complaints to the Railroad Commission, which had the authority to inspect the questioned wells. The Board had little interest in Humble's proposed civil suits against deviators, but would be interested in prosecuting criminal charges. (6)

Local law enforcement was not pursuing slant-hole drillers with the diligence expected by Humble Oil's field management. The company brought in "Special Ranger" investigators to build cases against the deviators. (7)

Special Ranger J. D. Matthews (Doug) questioned Pete Long's field hand Leonard R. Dorsey on the night of July 25, 1961, in the Woodlawn Motel in Henderson. The interrogation got ugly, and Matthews, claiming Dorsey pulled out a knife, shot and killed Dorsey. Matthews was arrested and indicted for murder on September 5. (8)

Humble Oil could not afford to have its investigator Matthews convicted of murder in the killing of Dorsey. Knowing of the hostility toward Humble, which was exacerbated by the killing, Humble needed the best local lawyers to defend their man. The company asked Fred Erisman to defend Matthews at trial. Erisman agreed to defend Matthews *if* Humble would provide him access to its files related to the slant-hole matter. Erisman, with access to Humble's files, now had a clear view of Humble's perspective if the company chose to pursue his friend John Wrather for stealing oil from the company with illegally slanted wells. Based on my studies of Erisman's actions in his defense of the deviators, I don't believe he needed any help from Humble's files.

The drilling of these three deviated wells—two by Long and one by Barber—into producing wells owned by Humble and Shell should have sent a loud message to anyone concerned with the East Texas Oil Field. These incidents, coupled with Matthews's killing of Dorsey, all occurring in 1961, could not have been kept secret.

In addition to the incidents just noted, the Railroad Commission lost two of its three commissioners in 1961. Olin Culberson, who had served as a Railroad Commissioner since his election in 1940, had been an outspoken champion of independent oilmen, and had brought important changes to the commission. He insisted on appointing graduate petroleum engineers instead of political friends to the commission staff. He, along with Bill Murray, insisted that casinghead gas be recovered instead of being flared. Culberson died on June 22, 1961.

Governor Price Daniel appointed Ben Ramsey, a six-term lieutenant governor, to replace Culberson on September 18. Ramsey was a respected (conservative) politician, but had little experience or knowledge of the affairs of the commission.

Ernest Thompson became ill in 1960, but retained his seat on the commission, although absent, until he finally retired in 1965. The Colonel died in Amarillo on June 28, 1966.

The loss of Culberson and Thompson and the appointment of a second rookie regulator Byron Tunnell, to replace Thompson, just as the slant-hole matter was emerging left the commission with Murray to handle the developing scandal essentially alone. (9)

NOTES

1. The Tobin and Anne Armstrong Research Center at the Texas Rangers Hall of Fame and Museum in Waco, Texas, contains a treasure trove of books, documents, and artifacts that provide an excellent history of the legendary Texas Rangers. Thanks to the hospitality of Rusty Bloxom, the center's Research Librarian, I spent December 4, 5, and 6, 2018, reading the reports in each of the 61 well-organized folders that cover the Rangers' investigations of the "Slant-Hole Scandal." I shall refer to these reports, most of them written from Ranger Jim Ray to Ranger Capitan Bob Crowder during the Ranger's 1962-63 investigations. I shall refer to these documents throughout this book as follows: "Rangers Folder #, (date of report)."

2. Rangers Folder #2, undated, but reportedly delivered to the Railroad Commission sometime before June 21, 1961, tells of Long 's drilling into Humble's wells.

3. The facts of the Nortex episode reported here come from (a) the Report of the House General Investigating Committee, pp. 15 and 16, (b) articles

that appeared in the *Longview Daily News* and *The Dallas Morning News* during the period from May 15 through August 15, 1962, and (c) a personal interview conducted by the author in Houston on October 16, 2010, with Ms. Risa Ray, who had been secretary to the secretary-treasurer of Nortex, J. P. Broxson, when Nortex purchased the package of slanted wells in 1961.

4. Rangers Folders #2, #3 (5/1/61), and #4 (5/26/61).

5. In this case, Barber's well had been producing in the middle of the field, but by 1961, the encroachment of water from the west had decreased its oil production to nearly zero. Barber, hoping to reestablish oil production, redrilled his well deviated to the east and into the remaining pool of oil.

6. Rangers Folder # 5 (5/26/61)

7. Ranger Glenn Elliott explained to me that railroads and major oil companies experienced internal theft on a large scale and were permitted to appoint "Special Rangers" to conduct intra-company investigations. They were allowed to carry weapons, but could not make arrests. They were paid by their employers and not by the State of Texas.

8. *Longview Daily News*, July 27, 1961.

9. David F. Prindle, *Petroleum Politics and the Texas Railroad Commission,* University of Texas Press, Austin, TX 1981, p. 88.

Bill Murray knew he had to act. The incidents of 1961, especially the killing of Dorsey by an employee of the hated Humble Oil, required some action by the Railroad Commission.

Murray had concluded in January 1962 that the deviators would want their wells classified as marginal to maximize their ill-gotten gains. He hired an engineering graduate student at the University of Texas at Austin to examine the records of nearly 4,000 marginal wells in search of those with little or no decline in production over several years. Murray presented his list of several hundred suspicious wells to Attorney General Will Wilson's office and asked for an investigation. The response was, "the attorney general could not authorize such a fishing expedition and that he should come back when he had evidence instead of inferences." (1), (2) That Murray, never a political animal, and Wilson, a consummate political climber, had little use for each other became clear to me in my review of the slant-hole matter.

Wilson's political ambition was the governor's office, but when Lyndon Johnson's seat in the U.S. Senate became vacant upon his becoming vice president, Wilson joined *seventy* others in a special election in April 1961 for the vacated seat. He finished fourth, but retained his office as attorney general. Allen Duckworth, writing for *The Dallas Morning News*, noted in August 1961 that Wilson had already been running for governor unofficially, so as to avoid reporting requirements for official candidates. (3,) (4), (5)

Walter Lee Snyder, Matthews' stepbrother, was the third person present in the Woodlawn Motel on that fateful July night in 1961 when Matthews interviewed Leonard R. Dorsey. But Snyder had taken a job with An-Son Drilling Company of Colombia, in South America, and was unavailable, because of government restrictions, to testify at trial in the

United States until he had spent four months in foreign employment. Because of Snyder's inability to return from Colombia to Henderson and Erisman's busy trial schedule, the court rescheduled Matthews's trial from November 27, 1961, to February 12, 1962.

Testimony at trial showed that Matthews shot Dorsey with a .38 caliber pistol, the slug passing through Dorsey's chest and lodging in the back of his chair. Matthews testified in his own defense: "I was sent up here (in March of 1961) to check trucks that might be hauling stolen oil off our leases, along with other investigations." Snyder testified that he did not actually see the shooting. He told the court that he took Dorsey, a 43-year-old veteran of World War II and an employee of Pete Long's who lived in Overton, to Kilgore. There they had a few beers before going to Matthews's room at the Woodlawn Motel in Henderson with a pint of whiskey. The confusing liquor laws in Texas, where each county determines whether to allow the sale of alcoholic beverages, left Rusk County (Henderson and half of Kilgore) dry and Gregg County (Longview and the other half of Kilgore) wet. Dorsey lived in Overton, partly in Rusk and partly in dry Smith County, leaving a trip to Gregg County necessary for the purchase of beer and whiskey. There is no evidence that either Matthews or Snyder had met Dorsey before the fatal night's interview.

Both Matthews and Snyder testified that they were investigating directional drilling and other matters in Rusk, Gregg, and Upshur counties. Snyder said that Matthews and Dorsey discussed directional drilling and the transfer of production to dummy wells. He also said that Dorsey told them that he had a lot of information that he was willing to give if he were paid for it. Snyder testified that Matthews claimed to have no money, but he might put Dorsey in touch with someone who would pay him.

The conversation continued and the question of Dorsey's testifying in court arose, which angered Dorsey. At that point, according to Snyder, Dorsey called Matthews a stool pigeon, and after a scuffle Dorsey departed. There was no testimony about where Dorsey went or how he went or for how long. He had no vehicle of his own that night, so he must have walked, but not far. Snyder then said that he was in the bathroom and heard a conversation indicating Dorsey had returned. He heard Dorsey threaten to kill Matthews.

The shooting occurred at that point, and Dorsey fell into the bathroom, according to Snyder. Matthews had testified earlier that he shot only when Dorsey came at him with a knife. The newspaper reporter mistakenly stated that the prosecution—surely, it was the defense—presented a knife it claimed to have been clutched in Dorsey's hand when his body was found. (6) Dorsey's brother Jimmy testified that Dorsey had lost his knife on a fishing trip to Texarkana and that he had never seen his brother with such a knife as the one presented in court as Dorsey's. Ranger Elliott, who was present at the trial, told me, "Both the deceased and the defendant were pretty rough boys, and Dorsey's brothers were expected to be a bit unruly." Elliott had been present to ensure the absence of any disturbance in the court.

Judge Joe C. Gladney read the charge to the jury at 1:45 p.m. on February 14, 1962, and gave each side one hour to sum up. The jury got the case at 3:45 p.m. and returned its verdict at 4:45 p.m. Foreman Floyd Holland read the verdict: "Not guilty."

During my research for this book, I read the reports of the case in the *Longview Daily News* and concluded that both Matthews and Snyder lied under oath. (7), (8) If Matthews shot Dorsey in the chest and the bullet lodged in the back of Dorsey's chair, as claimed by the investigating officers at the scene, Dorsey must have been seated rather than lunging toward Matthews with a knife. If Dorsey fell into the bathroom, was he carrying the chair behind him? Dead men tell few tales, and we shall never know the truth in this case. Ranger Elliott, who died on the last day of 2012, suggested to me during my research that Snyder and Dorsey, and probably Matthews, all got drunk and the interview got out of hand.

Dorsey's family soon filed a civil suit against Humble Oil & Refining Company and others, which named both Doug Matthews and Walter Snyder as codefendants. This suit ended with a settlement on March 28, 1962, in which Humble paid the Dorseys $35,000. Gordon Wellborn and his partner Rex Houston represented the Dorsey family, and Fred Erisman and Frank Heard represented Humble as well as Matthews and Snyder. That the Dorseys settled their case against Humble for a mere $35,000 seems hard to believe when compared with settlements of the twenty-first century, but this sum was serious money for an oilfield worker's family in 1962.

In the last half of the twentieth century, under its highly respected director, Col. Homer Garrison, the Texas Rangers, a division of the Texas Department of Public Safety (DPS), was the pride of Texas. (9)

The DPS came into the slant-hole investigation on February 20, 1962, a year after the Pete Long and Bull Barber incidents. Gordon Rees and former State Judge Samuel Reams, both officers of Humble Oil, arrived quietly at DPS headquarters in Austin on that date to complain of slant-hole drilling in East Texas. Humble had already experienced Pete Long's drilling into their wells a year earlier, and having seen little or no clear action from the Railroad Commission, they went to the DPS. They reported that unscrupulous oilmen had drilled at least 300 oil wells at illegal angles to steal oil from neighboring leases, many of which were owned by Humble. Rees and Reams argued that these acts constituted a felony and asked for assistance in investigating the matter. Sam Reams had served as judge of the 79th State District Court, which covered Jim Wells, Duval, Brooks, and Starr counties, until his electoral defeat at age 43 in 1952. He joined the legal staff of Humble Oil shortly thereafter.

Humble had been conducting its own slant-hole investigations since at least 1961, when Matthews killed Dorsey. But this was Humble's first official complaint about slant-hole drilling.

Bill Kavanaugh, legal counsel to the DPS and Col. Garrison's administrative assistant, prepared an internal DPS report on February 23 that cited Texas law, including the Rule of Absolute Ownership and the Rule of Capture. (10)

Kavanaugh doubted that a case for felony theft could be successfully prosecuted and suggested basing cases on "conspiracy to steal" instead. He doubted that Texas law would authorize search warrants for the necessary tests on suspected wells to determine their illegal deviation. He advised Col. Garrison that the DPS should coordinate with local prosecuting attorneys, whose cooperation would be necessary for any successful prosecution.

Kavanaugh preferred that DPS officers remain on the sidelines because civil suits against them for false accusations could ruin the officers and the DPS. He wanted the DPS to avoid any involvement in the matter. But if the DPS were to enter the issue, it should be done through the counties' grand juries, with the first accusations made by those bodies. He also stated that the slant-hole matter would present "cases of first impression"; that is, cases for which the courts would plow new ground in deciding the issues in question.

Kavanaugh clearly wanted nothing to do with this hot potato. He knew the deviators might turn politicians against the DPS to avoid the presumed legal consequences of their thefts. The Rangers would then be at risk of legislative retribution, as well as personal lawsuits. The accused deviators had ample political clout, and the local grand juries, prosecutors, and petit jurors would be reluctant to attack their friends and neighbors.

Col. Garrison, however, decided the Texas Rangers should investigate the slant-hole matter with Captain Bob Crowder in charge of the investigations. Once ordered into battle by Col. Garrison, the Rangers began an aggressive and detailed investigation, as was their tradition.

A group that included Kavanaugh, Railroad Commission Chairman Bill Murray, Col. Garrison, and Ranger Capt. Bob Crowder met on Tuesday, April 3, in Col. Garrison's office to discuss the recent cases in which the commission had found evidence of the illegal drilling of directional wells.

Murray informed the group that new commission rules required a survey of any well that deviated more than three degrees from the vertical. There had been several instances of falsified surveys on excessively slanted wells, as determined by surveys run by the commission, but no penalties had been assessed.

Murray also told the group shortly after the meeting ended that he had told neither his own attorney nor the attorney general's office of any of the matters they had discussed. Maybe he just forgot that in January, Attorney General Will Wilson, no political ally of Murray's, had rebuffed his request for an investigation of wells Murray thought to be illegally deviated. Nor did he tell them of the letter he received from Ed Stanley in April 1950, or of his January 1962 research project with a UT graduate student who looked for a decline in the production of marginal wells.

He also told them that the commission had begun to investigate leases that were predominantly marginal, thinking that operators who would abuse the Marginal Well Rule on one lease would do so on others.

The commission found that Amtex Oil owned approximately 20 wells classified as marginal in the Thomas Johnson survey on the western side of the field. The easternmost well, deviated to the east, had produced all the oil for the entire lease, some 300 barrels per day. (11) No well, proratable or marginal, in the East Texas Oil Field was permitted to produce more than 20 barrels of oil per day.

Crowder drafted Ranger Jim Ray, whose area of responsibility included the East Texas field, as his man in charge of local on-the-ground investigations in the "slant-hole" matter.

Ray, in his second of many reports to Bob Crowder, dated April 11, 1962, reported that Murray had named commission engineers L. Dwight Murphy and Robert W. Matthews and field men Nelson Decker and Henry J. Stewart as suspects in probable payoffs for falsifying directional survey and production reports for deviators. Then, he reported that common talk in Gregg County indicated that Railroad Commissioners were accepting bribes from deviators, with a going price of $5,000 per deviated well. (12)

The big news, apparently missed by the Rangers and by General Wilson, was that Jim Drummond, a reporter for *Oil Daily*, had called Chairman Murray on Monday, April 10, to ask about rumors of slant-hole drilling in East Texas. Drummond's report on the following day in his paper stated that Murray confirmed his knowledge of slant-hole drilling in East Texas and his futile efforts to stop it. (13) It was not until *The Dallas Morning News* published articles on April 21, and 27, 1962, that the criminal enterprise became general knowledge statewide. (14), (15)

NOTES

1. David F. Prindle reported in his 1981 book *Petroleum Politics and the Texas Railroad Commission*, p.90, that Bill Murray gave him a copy of a memo written by Murray dated July 2, 1962 (well after the attorney general's investigation had been launched.) There was no addressee given, but Murray probably wrote the memo to his own diary or files. The memo recorded his attempts to determine which wells had been illegally deviated and by whom. I asked the commission for a copy of the Murray memo but was told the commission had no copy.

2. I emailed Professor Prindle at the University of Texas-Austin on May 9, 2007, and asked him to share the Murray memo with me. He responded, "Damn! I knew this would happen." He told me that the Government Department had moved across campus and that he had destroyed all the Murray memos, saying to himself, "Nobody has wanted to look at this material since 1979. But I bet I'll get an email in a few months... And this happened."

3. Allen Duckworth, "POLITICS 1961 – Among Big Six, A Triple Split", *The Dallas Morning News*, March 26, 1961, p. 15.

4. Allen Duckworth, "POLITICS 1961- Two Races Start Up", *The Dallas Morning News*, August 10, 1961, p 13.

5. At the time, the governor, lieutenant governor, and attorney general served two-year terms.

6. *Longview Daily News*, February 15, 1962.

7. *Longview Daily News*, July 27, 1961; February 14 and 15, 1962. I also have copies of all the court documents filed in this case.

8. *Longview Daily News*, February 14, 1962.

9. The Texas Department of Public Safety is an autonomous agency of the state and is not controlled by or related to the Office of the Attorney General.

10. Rangers Folder # 6, (2/21/62), Garrison to Kavanaugh; 2/23/62, Kavanaugh to Garrison.

11. Rangers Folder #9 (4/3/62). Kavanaugh's lengthy (6 pages) report states, "On the east most well there had been a work over rig deviated to the west [sic] and produced all of the oil for the whole lease. The lease had gone from almost zero production to 300 barrels per day." Surely the well was deviated to the east into the remaining oil instead of west into salt water.

12. Rangers Folder #11 (4/11/62) Ray to Crowder.

13. James Drummond, Oil Daily, April 11, 1962.

14. Richard M. Morehead, "Crooked Holes: Oil Thieves Work a New Angle", *The Dallas Morning News*, April 21, 1962, p. 8. This is the first report of slant-hole drilling in Texas that I could find after Drummond's April 11, 1962, article in *Oil Daily*.

15. Austin Bureau of the News, "East Texas Well Owners Face Slant-Hole Surveys" *The Dallas Morning News*, April 27, 1962, p. 10.

The Rangers played important roles in the slant-hole investigation.

Captain Robert A. "Bob" Crowder, born in 1901 in the tiny village of Minden, 10 miles south of Henderson, knew East Texas well. He entered law enforcement as a Dallas policeman in 1925 after having served as a U.S. Marine in World War I. He joined the newly-created Texas Highway Patrol and served in the DPS Bureau of Intelligence.

The Texas Rangers appointed Crowder to Ranger Company B in 1939. He rose to Acting Chief of the Texas Rangers in 1956 but quickly became frustrated with administrative duty. He preferred action. He moved back into the ranks of the Rangers in 1960 and became captain of Company B in Dallas. Col. Garrison once observed, "I have heard it said that the Texas Rangers are the Marines of Texas law enforcement. If so," pointing at Crowder, "there goes my top Marine." Bob Crowder believed that a man must prove himself before becoming a Ranger, who he defined as "an officer who is able to handle any situation without definite instructions from his commanding officer or higher authority. This ability must be proven before a man becomes a Ranger."

In April 1955, 81 inmates of the Rusk State Hospital took over Wards 6 and 8, attacked three trustees and two attendants, and took the unit physician, the assistant supervisor, and the hospital superintendent hostage. Bob Crowder arrived at the facility alone. After assessing the situation, he agreed to talk with the inmates. He warned them he was coming in armed because he was unwilling to become a hostage. During the next 20 minutes, Crowder reasoned with the inmates and assured them of a fair hearing of their grievances. He then ordered them to release their hostages and surrender their weapons. The inmates complied and the incident ended peacefully.

Bob Crowder tolerated no disrespect, and his men held him in high esteem. They said he was easy to work for. He was tough, but always fair. My late friend Ranger Glenn Elliott told me of his great respect for Crowder, who died of a heart attack on November 26, 1972, in Dallas. (1)

Jim Ray, like his boss Bob Crowder, was a native East Texan, born in tiny Bullard near Tyler in 1914. He attended Bullard High School, and after starting college at Stephen F. Austin State Teachers College, graduated from East Texas State Teachers College with a degree in business administration in 1940.

In November 1941, he started recruit training school for the DPS, but was drafted into the U.S. Army the day after Christmas. Ray shipped out to the Pacific theater in early 1943 and became known as a "real hell-raiser." After one particularly brutal assault on New Guinea in early 1943, the Army sent Ray to Officer's Candidate School in Brisbane, Australia. He returned to New Guinea as a 2nd Lieutenant and Platoon Leader, a post that put him first off the landing barge for five more landings. Ray lived through several fights to the death with the Japanese before being sent to Hot Springs, Arkansas, in May 1945. There he recovered from malaria, pneumonia, dysentery, and a malignant growth on his lip. His discharge arrived on November 24, 1945.

Ray's return to the DPS as a Highway Patrolman lasted until the Army recalled him as a captain in 1950 during the conflict in Korea. He remained stateside as a trainer. In April 1957, Ray joined the other 41 Texas Rangers and served under Bob Crowder. (2) He retired from the Rangers in 1969 when he became Chief of the new Public Safety Criminal Law Enforcement Division. (3) Ray died in 2003 at age 89. Glenn Elliott's love and respect for Ray was evidenced when the usually shy Elliott delivered the eulogy at Ray's funeral.

Glenn Elliott was the only Texas Ranger I ever knew personally. I described our first meeting in the Introduction. Our second meeting was in 1983 when my son William, then an early teenager and neophyte driver, and driving alone, wrecked my car at a slick intersection in Longview. I had just arrived at my parent's house unaware of the wreck, to find my dad in a hurry to leave. He instructed me to "Get in the car!" He had just received a phone call from Ranger Elliott, a close personal friend with instructions to come to his house immediately because William had been in a wreck, but was unhurt.

We arrived at Elliot's house, the one closest to the intersection where the wreck occurred. William was there, shaken and embarrassed, but safe. Once Ranger Elliott had determined William had not been injured, he protected the boy from local police, telling them, "This boy is my prisoner."

Over the years until Glenn's death on New Year's Eve 2012, he and I remained close friends.

Glenn was born on August 1, 1926, in the tiny community of Flag Springs near Windom, Texas, in Fannin County. The village lies near the Red River and at the time was home to 389 persons. Sam Rayburn, former Speaker of the U.S. House of Representatives, had been born in a house just across the road from Elliott's birth house. Elliott turned 18 in 1944 and was finally able to enlist for World War II. By the time he had finished training he was assigned to the MPs and stationed in occupied Japan. After his return from Japan and a stint as a utility lineman, he joined the Texas Highway Patrol in April 1949, and was assigned to the Longview District. In 1956, Glenn wrote to Garrison seeking an appointment to the Rangers, but didn't get the job.

Lone Star Steel, 30 miles north of Longview, experienced a wildcat strike in September and October 1957. The Texas Rangers, having been impressed by Elliott's work during the strike, made Elliott a Special Texas Ranger to work with Ranger Jim Ray. The strikers blew up the main gas line to the City of Pittsburg, thinking they were blowing up the gas line that fed the Lone Star plant. Colonel Homer Garrison commended Elliott for his service at the strike in a letter dated December 12, 1957.

In 1961, with a bigger budget, the Rangers increased the force from 52 to 62. Glenn was among those selected. He was assigned to Company B where Bob Crowder was his Captain. Glenn spent the next 26 years on active duty with the Rangers. During this time, he always tried to reason with the men he was arresting. They usually saw the wisdom of cooperation. Those who didn't ended up hurt, arrested, or dead. With his friend Bobby Nieman, Glenn co-authored two books in which he tells of his life and his experiences as a lawman. (4), (5)

NOTES

1. See http://www.texasranger.org/halloffame/Crowder_Bob.htm for a biography of Bob Crowder.

2. For a biography of Jim Ray, see http://www.texasranger.org/E-Books/ Oral History - Ray, Jim.pdf. The Texas Rangers comprise six companies that cover six delineated areas of the state. Each individual Ranger is responsible for one or more counties within his company's territory.

3. See http://www.texasranger.org/wp-content/uploads/2018/03/OBIT-Ray_ Jim.pdf.

4. Glenn Elliott and Robert Nieman, *Glenn Elliott: A Ranger's Ranger*, Texian Press, Waco, TX, 1999.

5. Glenn Elliott and Robert Nieman, *Glenn Elliott: Still a Ranger's Ranger*, Ranger Press, Longview, TX, 2002. My autographed copy of this book has disappeared.

Will Wilson came into the slant-hole matter long after he should have known about it. Humble Oil had initiated its own investigation after Pete Long had drilled into two of its well in January and March 1961. Shell Oil had complained to the Railroad Commission's Kilgore office of Bull Barber's drilling his Goyne well into its B. F. Laird well in April 1961. Humble's investigator Doug Matthews had killed Leonard Dorsey in July 1961. The DPS, in the form of the Texas Rangers, entered the fray on February 20, 1962. Jim Drummond's article in *Oil Daily* appeared on April 11, 1962. And the *The Dallas Morning News* published its first article on deviated wells on April 22, 1962.

Wilson suddenly discovered the slant-hole matter in late April, probably after reading *The Dallas Morning News* of April 22, and after Col. Garrison had ordered the Rangers into action. He likely did not see the article in *Oil Daily* of April 11. He had recently filed to run for governor in the Democratic primary election to be held on Saturday, May 5, 1962. He planned to ride his vigorous investigations of Billie Sol Estes's fraudulent dealings, his cleaning up of Galveston's gambling and prostitution, and his battle for the Texas Tidelands into the governor's mansion. But in January 1962, he had had no interest in Murray's concerns about slant-hole drilling. Once the story was made public, however, Wilson charged forward with vigor to bring the deviators to justice. But with only 13 days between the April 22 story in *The Dallas Morning News* and the May 5 Democratic Primary, he had little time to carve another notch on his gun for the prosecution of the deviators to his list of accomplishments.

Wilson devotes forty-four lines of his 238-page memoir to the slant-hole matter. He states on page 158 and 159:

"When I became Attorney General [1957], the [East Texas] field was some 26 years old, an old field, and certain individual operators were rumored to have been drilling slanted holes from dry areas, tapping into productive leases higher up strata. Some of those wells were said to be bottomed as much as a mile or two from their tops and on someone else's property. Theft was what it was, theft of oil-or 'hot oil,' as the press dubbed it. Humble Oil Co., now ExxonMobil, came to me with a suspicion that people with 'metal straws' were sucking oil from other people's leases.

'Well, we'll just find out,' I told them." (1), (2), (3), (4)

Ranger Jim Ray reported that at a meeting of Rangers and commission personnel on April 19, Bill Murray proposed a plan for sending letters to suspected deviators asking for responses. "Murray indicated that the above action would take approximately three weeks and that it was probably the best that it did as final action in this matter would come after election date [May 5]." (5)

Ray interviewed two confidential informants, William Brumley and Don Baker, on April 25. These two, partners in Oil Capital Drilling Company headquartered in Kilgore, admitted they drilled many of the crooked wells in the East Texas Oil Field. Humble, clearly knowing of the slant-hole drilling activity from among other indications, its participation in the drilling of the Boy Scout Well in 1949, and Brumley signed a contract of unstated date, probably in 1958 or 1959, in which Humble agreed to pay Brumley handsomely for his work:

- $1,000 per month for 10 months
- $1,500 per crooked well for the first 10 wells for which he provided information
- $1,000 per well for information on the next 20 crooked wells
- $750 for information on each of the other crooked wells
- 10 percent of all monies recovered by Humble in civil suits against deviators, up to a total of $350,000
- Humble's protection from violence as well as from civil and criminal litigation.

The oil company persuaded Brumley to convince Baker to agree to the same terms. Brumley did so, and signed a contract with Humble in November 1959. He had given affidavits to Humble in which he named deviators, leases, names of engineers, and drilling companies that were involved. Those documents remain secret and are likely now lost in the Exxon Mobil company archives or destroyed. I did not seek any information from any major oil company in my research for this book. I chose to allow those sleeping dogs to lie rather than stir up a potential hornet's nest and get hurt. We saw in Chapter 13 that one of Humble's investigators shot and killed a deviator's field man.

The informants reported that a "combine" of deviators had collected $100,000 at $100 per deviated well to retain attorneys who would advise and defend the deviators as well as pay off directional engineers. (6)

Ray interviewed B. J. Hallmark of Schlumberger on April 27 in Tyler. Hallmark told Ray that he had never falsified any surveys of wells. He also said he had refused deals offered him on many occasions to falsify Schlumberger's well surveys. He refused to give Ray a statement without first conferring with Schlumberger's attorneys, and noted that company policy dictates client information remains confidential. Ray told Schlumberger that his reports to clients had been sent via registered mail, and that such mailing of false reports is a violation of postal regulations. The confidential informants, however, insisted Schlumberger had definitely run surveys on deviated wells.

Ray interviewed Robert S. Beatty, Schlumberger's district manager in Tyler, the next day. He told Beatty that two of his employees, Hallmark and J. C. Connally, had made surveys on known or suspected deviated wells. He made sure that Beatty understood the company could be dragged into a lawsuit if his engineers had falsified a report. Beatty said none of his employees would falsify reports, and if they did, they would be fired. He also assured Ray that Schlumberger would cooperate if its legal counsel approved. (7), (8)

My father's files revealed that Carter-Jones Drilling Company drilled his illegally-deviated Albert Castleberry #1 well. Schlumberger's Hallmark ran the directional survey and certified the well to be straight. A later

survey by the commission revealed the well to be deviated. Hallmark had
lied to Ranger Ray.

On the same day, Howard Goodwin, an investigator hired by the
deviators, called Ray. After Goodwin felt he had confidence in Ray,
he began to tell Ray about the activities of the deviators. He told of
meetings in Tyler with deviators Bill Bowie, H. L. "Pete" Long, W. S.
"Bull" Barber, Jake Maxwell, E. W. "Jelly" Scates, and others on April 25
and 26. He told Ray that he did not condone the actions of the deviators,
and that they were no doubt guilty of theft. His job was to find facts that
would mitigate the damage to the deviators. He had already found one of
Humble's deviated wells and expected to find more, but Humble and the
other majors had already "cleaned up their mess and were now trying to
pin the whole directional drilling fiasco on those little independents left."
He, Goodwin, would try to dig up information with which to blackmail,
in particular, Bill Murray. (9)

At last, it was May 5 and the primary elections were at hand. In the
six-man race for governor, Wilson came in fourth with only 12 percent
of the votes. Governor Price Daniel, the incumbent seeking a fourth
term, was third, and General Edwin Walker, the John Bircher, had the
fewest votes at 10 percent. John Connally and Don Yarborough were
the top two vote-getters and faced off in the runoff election on June
2, which Connally barely won. Connally faced Republican Jack Cox, the
former 1960 Democratic candidate for governor, in the general election
in November. After a tough race, Connally became governor, and
Wilson, with his political rise curtailed by his defeat in the gubernatorial
primary, became a lame duck. Nonetheless, he didn't allow the defeat to
diminish the vigor of his pursuit of the deviators. If anything, Wilson
exerted greater energy to that cause. (10)

NOTES

1. Will R. Wilson, with Jack Keever, and Anita Howard, *The Will to Win*, privately printed, 2008. Linward Shivers, an assistant attorney general in Wilson's office, gave me a copy of Wilson's memoir when I interviewed him at his home in Austin.

2. Wilson's report is surprising for a trained geologist. None of the slanted wells went into productive leases "higher up strata," and none reached "two miles" from its surface location.

3. Wilson says he contacted, Ben Ramsey, a new member of the Railroad Commission in September 1961, about the slant-hole matter.

4. Wilson continues, "The Humble people also talked to Commissioner Ramsey, and we arranged to seize some big wells which were located among stripper-or marginal-wells, which were shallow wells producing more water than oil. And maybe a particular well was inexplicably producing large quantities of oil."

5. Rangers Folder # 13, (4/21/62), Ray to Crowder.

6. Rangers Folder # 14, (4/26/62), Ray to Crowder.

7. Rangers Folder # 15, (5/1/62), Ray to Crowder.

8. I discussed the slant-hole affair with Bill Maxwell, son of W. T. (Tommy) Maxwell, who had been a partner in Carter-Jones Drilling Company and in Amtex Oil Company. Bill told me that Schlumberger ran all the logging equipment and prepared all the logs for all the crooked wells and that Phil Gaines doctored those logs so that they appeared to be from legitimate wells. He also told me that after the scandal was over, Schlumberger fired Gaines. Personal interview with Bill Maxwell at the Cherokee Club on May 2, 2013. Bill told me that Carter-Jones and Amtex drilled more deviated wells than anyone else.

9. Ranger Folder # 15, (5/1/62), Ray to Crowder, Confidential Information attached to the Report.

10. *The Dallas Morning News* publishes annual editions of *Texas Almanac* in which one can find almost any fact regarding the state. I have taken these election data from the 2006-2007 edition. These almanacs are distributed by Texas A&M University Press Consortium, College Station, TX 77843-4354; www.texasalmanac.com

Texas Highway Patrolman Errett Hale contacted an informant who said he'd worked on deviated wells and would take Rangers to those leases. Ray, Hale, and DPS Special Agent George Read were meeting in Henderson on Tuesday morning May 8 with the informant, Roy Carlyle, when Col. Garrison summoned him and Reed to Austin for a 3 p.m. meeting with Bill Murray and commission personnel. The assembled officers decided to call the four commission employees suspected of complicity in the theft— Murphy, Matthews, Decker, and Stewart—to Austin for polygraph tests the next day, two in the morning, and two in the afternoon.

Murray summoned Matthews and Murphy to Austin. Matthews confessed his involvement and expressed his regret. Murray fired him effective May 15. Murphy wanted to confer with his attorney before agreeing to a polygraph test. Murray failed to call Decker and Stewart because "he had been too busy talking to the other two." Ray and Reed were angry with Murray for his failure to do as he had promised, and became suspicious that Murray, himself, might be involved in a cover-up. Their suspicion was enhanced because the Rangers had already heard rumors that Murphy had carried suitcases full of money to the commission in Austin. (1), (2)

Back in Tyler, Stewart convinced the Rangers of his innocence and agreed to a polygraph test. Decker, a political appointee at the commission and a personal friend of Murray's, was angry and insisted that "everyone was being double-crossed by the people in Austin." He refused to talk until he had spoken with his attorney, Foster Bean, and refused a polygraph test. It became clear later that he was a part of the slant-hole conspiracy.

With Matthews' confession and Stewart's apparent innocence, only Murphy and Decker remained as suspects. The angry Decker told the Rangers that Murray should be subjected to the polygraph; Murray readily agreed. Murray's agreement convinced the surprised Rangers that Murray was innocent, but that Col. Garrison needed to apply continuous pressure to keep Murray moving forward. (3)

Ray and Ranger Louis Rigler interviewed Robert Beatty, District Manager of Schlumberger Well Servicing Company in Tyler on May 14. Beatty refused to give the officers any information before conferring with counsel. Schlumberger's counsel, Kent Pritchard, said that the company would cooperate with the investigation if they could do so without violating company policy of keeping client information confidential. Beatty specifically refused to identify employees who worked on logging truck #2520, which the Rangers suspected of surveying deviated wells.

That same afternoon, Ray found Luther McClendon who had worked on truck #2520. McClendon said persons unknown to him had advised him not to tell anyone about Schlumberger's business. McClendon said he had ordered Phil Gaines, another Schlumberger employee, to leave his property and to stay away. He also explained to the Rangers how Schlumberger personnel had doctored logs of deviated wells so they would appear normal. (4), (5)

Brumley and Baker, already identified as informants, told the Rangers that Bill Murray had met on May 14 with attorneys Angus Wynne, Gordon Wellborn, Fred Weeks, Foster Bean, and Fred Erisman. These lawyers asked Murray to permit deviators to plug and abandon their deviated wells on the eastside of the East Texas field without requiring directional surveys. A show cause hearing scheduled at the commission for the following day to deal with this proposal apparently convened in private. The commission granted the requested permission in a directive which would be dated May 18. By early morning May 16, operators were calling Roy Payne in Kilgore requesting plugging permits. Within a week Payne had received 33 applications for plugging permits covering 120 wells. Paine held them all, pending receipt of sealed instructions from Austin, and asked Ray to be present for the opening of those orders. The May 18 directive is clearly not one of force; it leaves too many outs for the suspected deviators. Again, Murray's commitment to the investigation appeared weak. (6), (7)

An unhappy Col. Garrison convened another meeting in Austin on May 22 in response to Murray's directive of May 18. Those assembled were Garrison's assistant Bill Kavanaugh, AG Wilson and his assistant Houghton Brownlee, Murray and his engineers Arthur Barbeck and George Singletary, and Ranger Ray.

Wilson and Garrison criticized the commission's directive of May 18 because its orders were in conflict with those issued a year earlier. The investigators saw Murray's new orders as a "half-hearted attempt by someone to permit illegal oil operators in the East Texas oil field to cover up some of their wrongdoing." The assembly eventually decided to require directional surveys on all wells on which inclination surveys had shown deviation greater than the allowed three degrees from the vertical. (8), (9)

E. M. Fisk's application to plug two wells on his L. McCord lease, which was adjacent to a Sinclair Oil lease, raised Ray's interest. Both of Fisk's wells were producing 14 barrels daily for 30 days per month under their classification as marginal wells. The Sinclair wells were "full allowable" wells prorated at 20 barrels per day for eight days per month, except for one five-barrel-per-day well very near Fisk's wells. That Fisk wanted to plug his two wells that made a total of 840 barrels per month, while each of Sinclair's full allowable wells made only 160 barrels, made it relatively clear they were deviated wells, bottomed under Sinclair's lease. Roy Payne called the commission's Austin office on May 24 to notify the commission of Fisk's obviously deviated wells and his application to plug them. The next day, Fred Young, the commission's attorney, called Payne telling him to grant Fisk permission to plug his wells. Both Payne and Ray were livid with Murray's continuing to vacillate between apparent cooperation with the investigation and covering for the deviators. (10)

Then, on May 26, Murray instructed Payne to reinstate all severed pipeline connections and allowables with no explanation. And, three days later, Murray instructed Payne to run inclination surveys on any wells selected by the DPS, and, furthermore, to ignore any protests of plugging applications. Payne got another call the next day instructing him not to mail any further letters to suspected deviators. Payne was confused.

Gordon Rees, a Humble investigator, told Ray that Continental Oil had agreed to a settlement with deviator Billy Bridewell. Continental's attorney confirmed that he had settled its claim against Bridewell for a payment of $200,000. The lawyer explained that Bridewell was the son-in-law of respected Tyler judge Fred Weeks, and Continental wanted to avoid embarrassing Weeks. Weeks was also among the attorneys representing the deviators.

Ray learned on Wednesday morning, May 30, that Ed Stanley had junked five of his suspected wells by dropping sucker rods, tubing, and cement into the well's casing. Surveying these wells was now impossible. Yes, this is the same Ed Stanley who as a commission engineer had written a letter to the commission warning of slant-hole drilling in 1950. (11)

Thus, May came to a close and the long-sought inclination surveys finally began on June 1.

Commission personnel moved a workover rig onto Mark Oil's M. C. Elliott lease to conduct the first official inclination survey of the investigation. Rangers Ray and Ernest Daniel were on hand to protect commission personnel from the potential violence threatened by some deviators. Even Attorney General Wilson, along with his assistants Houghton Brownlee and Linward Shivers, made appearances at some wells being surveyed. Wilson announced later that he had requested that 50 DPS officers be sent to East Texas while he sought blanket court orders for inspections of suspected wells. (12), (13)

Col. Garrison, along with his officers and Rangers, informed commissioner Murray on June 19 that the House General Investigating Committee, having been informed of the slant-hole activity, would likely hold hearings to consider legislative remedies. (14), (15)

Ray suspected more slant-hole drilling in the small Hawkins oil field that sits just north of the tiny town of Hawkins in Wood County, 30 miles west of Longview. He went to Quitman, the county seat, about 20 miles northwest of Hawkins, to search the deed records for evidence. He discovered that Gregg County Judge Earl Sharp was the operator of the B. O. Hamill lease on which suspected deviated wells had recently been plugged in violation of Railroad Commission orders. The illegal plugging resulted in General Wilson's filing suit against Sharp. Ray also found that commission engineer L. D. Murphy owned a small interest in the Hamill lease through his attorney J. W. Tyner, Trustee and that Tyler Bank & Trust also owned an interest. The bank's interest, according to Ray, violated banking regulations against banks owning "an interest in a speculation."

Finally, on June 29, Ray learned from oil company and commission personnel that Sperry Sun Drilling Services, Inc.,now a subsidiary of Halliburton Energy Services, Inc., had developed an instrument that was small enough to be lowered into a well through the tubing and that would give both inclination and direction of the hole. Such an instrument would now be used in surveying suspected wells because the bottom of the hole could be located with greater accuracy. Furthermore, removal of the two-inch tubing would not be required, thereby saving much time and expense. (16), (17)

NOTES

1.   Rangers Folder # 17, Report # 8 (5/12/62), Ray to Crowder.

2.   See Note #8, Chapter 16. Bill Maxwell told me in our interview that his family and the L. D. Murphy family were near neighbors in Kilgore. Bill said that his father, Tommy Maxwell, collected suitcases full of money from the deviators and gave them to Murphy for delivery to the commission in Austin. He also confirmed that Phil Gaines had been the Schlumberger employee who doctored logs of deviated wells.

3.   See Note #1, above.

4.   Deviated wells would be noticeably "deeper" as the hypotenuse of a right triangle. A well said to be 3,600 feet deep might contain as much as 4,000–5,000 feet of pipe. The log would show the actual depth before being altered.

5.   See Note #2 above

6.   Rangers Folder # 18, Report # 9 (5/16/62)

7.   Rangers Folder # 19, Report # 10 (5/26/62), Ray to Crowder. A copy of the May 18 directive is attached to this Report.

8.   Rangers Folder # 20, Report # 11 (5/25/62), Ray to Crowder. A list of Applications to Plug is attached to this Report.

9.   The early well surveys were capable only of showing angle of deviation, but Sperry Sun's survey tool could measure both angle and direction of deviation.

10. Rangers Folder # 21. Report # 12 (5/26/62), Ray to Crowder. (11) Ray's Reports # 10, 11,

11. Ranger Folder #24, Report # 13, (6/24/62), Ray to Crowder.

12. Rangers Folder #24, Report # 13 (6/24/62), Ray to Crowder.

13. Fred Pass, 'Rangers Called to Aid in Drilling Probe," *The Dallas Morning News*, June 3, 1962, p. 6; "FIFTY RANGERS CALLED TO ETEX OIL FIELD," *Longview Sunday News Journal*, June 3, 1962.

14. Rangers Folder #25, Letter from Ray to Garrison of June 27, 1962.

15. Rangers Folder #26, Information Report (6/29/62).

16. Rangers Folder #26, Supplemental Information Report (6/29/62).

17. The Eastman tool required removal of the tubing and the sucker rods from the suspect well because it wouldn't fit easily inside the tubing. Sucker rods are steel rods, threaded with male or female connectors, usually 25-30 feet in length, connect the pump jack at the surface with a downhole pump through the tubing, and had to be removed for well surveys with either Eastman or Sperry Sun tools.

CHAPTER 18
THE SIX-MILLION-DOLLAR SWINDLE

James Wendover must have been happy with his deal, in which his total cost seems to have been $7.8 million for property allegedly worth nearly $13 million. But his happiness was short-lived. The spring of 1962 was his worst nightmare.

In late May 1962, Humble Oil sued Nortex, and Davis, for theft by slanted wells on the leases just purchased by Nortex. Wendover was shocked. On Saturday, June 2, Nortex and Railroad Commission officials visited the Jacobs lease, where they found that someone had tampered with the wells. Wendover immediately complained to Dallas District Attorney Henry Wade, who filed charges against Davis for fraud on June 9 in the court of Justice of the Peace Glenn Byrd in Dallas. The complaint alleged that Davis, on or about February 10, 1961, did "unlawfully and fraudulently take $6,000,000 in money and stocks and debentures of the Nortex Oil Co." Davis disappeared immediately after instructing his attorneys, Fred Erisman and Gordon Wellborn, to file a suit against Nortex seeking $250,000 in damages for slander. He claimed that he was innocent of any theft and that the Nortex action sullied his good reputation.

As the Railroad Commission began to survey suspected slanted wells in May 1962, the eight East Texas leases just bought by Nortex were among the first to be examined, and, of course, the surveys identified many deviated and dummy wells. Gibson Drilling Company of Kilgore had drilled and completed the Jacobs well #2-A on March 1, 1958, for Trust Oil and Gas, owned by E. B. Hearne Sr. Commission engineer L. Dwight Murphy certified it as a marginal well at 15.24 barrels per day, but it was actually a deviated well that produced 67 barrels per day. It was later connected to dummy wells #3, #4, and #5. By early December 1958, the Jacobs lease was producing 2,000 barrels per month. Gibson, again working for Trust Oil, completed the second crooked Jacobs well, the #6A, on December 21, 1958. Hudnall, in advising Nortex, had told

Wendover and later the Byrd court that Davis had not drilled any crooked wells on the leases he evaluated. Hudnall's statement was true, but it was also misleading. Davis had bought the crooked wells from Trust Oil. Hudnall should not have been ignorant of the nature of these wells given his acknowledged expertise and proximity to the East Texas Oil Field.

Hearne acted as the directional driller as well as operator on these wells. Hearne sold Trust Oil to Elba Oil, which was owned by Davis, for $50,000 and then Davis included Elba in the package sold to Nortex. The Investigating Committee stated that of the 105 wells bought by Nortex, 17 were deviated, and most of them were drilled around 1958. Schlumberger provided false electric logs for each of the 17 wells.

Nortex paid Ebro $500,000 for the Jacobs lease with its two crooked wells and six dummies, and falsified directional surveys or electric logs for seven of the eight wells provided by Ebro. Nortex had also bought the seven-well Dorsey lease and the 18-well Holt lease. These leases also had falsified surveys provided by Schlumberger and HOMCO.

On June 13, two investigators from the Dallas district attorney's office, Nortex attorney Fritz Lyne, and a group of Texas Rangers examined the Jacobs lease, where they found several hundred feet of metal and plastic pipe, a time clock, and other equipment that, according to Lyne, made it possible for oil to flow illegally between wells and storage tanks. The leases bought by Nortex were productive and valuable only because of the illegal wells on them.

Davis reappeared on the evening of June 13, and refused to say where he had been.

The hearing before Judge Byrd ran Wednesday through Saturday, June 27–30. All the facts discussed here were brought out at the hearing, but on Friday, Judge Byrd announced, "As far as I am concerned, the state has failed to prove theft or any misrepresentation on Davis's part." He also said that he would recess the court at 2 p.m. on Saturday regardless of whether the hearing was finished, adding, "I'm going to barbecue some spareribs tomorrow afternoon."

On Saturday, Byrd found Davis not guilty and dismissed the charges against him. Davis wept and said, "I've never stolen anything from anybody in my life, and I have never drilled a crooked well." District

Attorney Wade declined to take the case to a grand jury without further evidence. Davis was surely aware of the crooked wells on the leases he bought and then sold to Nortex, yet he warranted clear title. Nortex and Wendover were left swindled, and Davis was the main swindler as well as a pretty good actor.

NOTES

1.   See Chapter 13, Note 4, for sources.

Ray's research in Quitman convinced him that commission employees Dwight Murphy and Nelson Decker had been receiving cash and small interests in some of the illegal wells from the deviator operators. Although the investigation was advancing, the Rangers discovered that the district attorneys of Gregg, Rusk, and Upshur Counties were not enthusiastic supporters of their pursuits, and needed some "attitude adjustment." (1)

Informant Bill Brumley had been living part time with his aunt in Oklahoma City during the summer of 1962. Because he feared he might encounter violence, he left his copy of the Humble contract with his aunt for safekeeping while he went to work in the oil fields near Corpus Christi. Brumley's aunt wrote to him that if he did not pay her $200 per week, she would sell the contract to a newspaper for publication. Brumley apparently told Gordon Rees, Humble's chief investigator, who then called Ranger Ray on July 7, 1962, and told him of the attempted blackmail, and that he (Rees) had contacted the Oklahoma Crime Bureau. Ranger Sgt. Lester H. Robertson joined Brumley and Rees for a trip to visit the aunt in Oklahoma City. They told her that she was subject to prosecution in Texas for attempted bribery and violation of postal regulations. She then gave up the document and remained silent.

By July 11, officers and commission personnel had severed 335 presumably deviated wells on 56 leases owned by 42 operators. These severances had removed almost 117,000 barrels of oil per month from field production. (2)

Then, the Legislature decided it needed to join the action. The General Investigating Committee of the Texas House of Representatives had been investigating the fixing of basketball scores by gamblers in the spring and summer of 1962. Two of the 21 referees of Southwest

Conference basketball games had been in cahoots with gamblers, mostly in Waco. They impacted the point spreads in several games during the 1961-1962 season, and helped their gambler friends to unstated sums of money. (3) But word of the growing scandal in the oil patch changed the legislative committee's focus, and they forgot about basketball. The committee had already "received requests early in 1962 to investigate reports of slanted wells, marginal well violations, and a suspected conspiracy involving operators, drilling contractors, third-party servicing companies, and Railroad Commission employees." Clements also noted, "As the investigation broadens, people in the Kilgore area have ceased joking about slant drilling. Until a few weeks ago, a popular local farewell was, 'See you later, deviator.'" (4)

The committee heard undisclosed testimony from Bill Murray in executive session in Austin on Saturday, July 14, after which, Rep. DeWitt Hale of the committee, spoke to reporters, including Olen Clements of the *Houston Chronicle*. Clements reported, "Murray gave the committee many interesting facts and he [Hale] said that the chief aim of the committee will be to try to find ways of correcting loopholes in the oil proration laws that have been exploited by some operators for years." Clements also stated, "Major companies, chief sufferers from the oil stealing—possibly because they own most [of the] leases—are said to have known about the slant-hole production for a long time. But for some reason they kept quiet about it until recently when the East Texas probe blew the lid off." I think the major reason for this silence lies in the majors' own complicity in the thefts, as will appear later in the story. The article further noted, "an undercover investigator had said that three commission employees had been tied to a $100,000 bribe in the East Texas slant-hole probe. 'We have got them nailed to the cross,' the investigator said. 'They split a $100,000 bribe between them.' But he refused to name the suspects." (5)

The committee decided to hold a public hearing concerning the slant-hole affair in Dallas beginning August 27. Texas Rangers would be ordered to serve subpoenas on suspected slant-hole operators and their accomplices at the commission and at the well servicing companies, each of whom would be asked to incriminate himself and others.

The commission then issued another set of directions for wells on which surveys had been run. If any well on a lease were shown to be deviated, all wells on that lease would be shut in and sealed. But then, any wells on such leases could be reinstated if after being surveyed they were shown to be straight.

General Wilson got serious when he instructed the state auditor and his team to prepare analyses of the financial affairs of the four commission employees previously identified as suspects, four Schlumberger employees, four Eastman employees, nine trustee accounts, five well surveying companies, the affiliates of Elba Oil, Nortex Oil, Amtex Oil, Crusader Oil, and Judge Earl Sharp. Wilson wanted the auditors to search the deed and mortgage records of Smith, Gregg, Upshur, Rusk, Cherokee, Wood, and Navarro Counties for interests any of the suspected commission personnel might own. These data would be available when the Investigating Committee questioned suspected deviators and accomplices. (6)

By late June, Ray had figured out that results of the Eastman and Sperry Sun Surveys would likely be different. He suggested that defense counsel for the deviators would surely claim that, given the differences in the surveys, no one could determine the location of a suspected well. This uncertainty would surely impact any prosecution against the deviators. (7)

In early August, Ray learned that, Pan American Oil, Stanolind Oil, and P. G. Lake, Inc. owned leases whereon deviated wells had been found. Now it became clear that some major companies had also been drilling deviated wells. (8), (9), (10)

As the heat of August descended upon East Texas, the deviators were getting more and more concerned, and their tempers were beginning to show. A field hand working for (suspected) deviator Pleas Dawson went a little bit too far. Ranger William T. Newberry, along with a commission field man, parked their car near one of Dawson's leases and walked to the lease to inspect a well. When they returned to the car, they found the spark plug wires missing. Several days later, Rangers stopped several of Dawson's men and found them carrying pistols. Capt. Crowder had had enough of such sport, and visited Dawson. Ray, in reporting the

Crowder–Dawson meeting, stated only, "A satisfactory understanding was reached by Captain Crowder and Dawson." (11) The misbehavior of Dawson's men ceased. See Chapter 15 to review Crowder's calming an explosive confrontation at the Rusk State Hospital.

As mid-August arrived, the Rangers got ready to serve subpoenas on deviators and other potential witnesses for the upcoming HGIC hearings, set for August 27, in Dallas. Capt. Crowder called Rangers Ray and L. H. Robertson to the Siesta Motel in Kilgore on Thursday evening, August 16. Crowder explained that the committee wanted the subpoenas served quickly and quietly to prevent the targeted persons' being forewarned, and thus avoiding service. Ray noted in his report of August 19 that some of the subpoenaed witnesses said they had been warned of subpoenas by Thursday afternoon. (12)

It was on Sunday morning, August 19, when I had my unforgettable encounter with Ranger Glenn Elliot, described in the Introduction. My parents returned that Thursday from their "fishing trip to Caddo Lake."

The Rangers were still serving, or attempting to serve, subpoenas on Thursday. That same day, Ray learned that the HGIC planned to expose Railroad Commission personnel involved in the slant-hole affair. The committee also asked Ray to gather names of drillers and roughnecks who had worked on deviated wells. (13)

NOTES

1. Rangers Folder # 27, Information Report (7/12/62) Ray to Crowder. At this point Ray called his reports "Information Reports" instead of numbered reports.

2. Rangers Folder # 28, Information Report (7/16/62) Ray to Crowder.

3. Texas Legislature, House of Representatives, General Investigating Committee, *Official report to the House of Representatives of the 58th Legislature of Texas*, v. 2, 1963; (http://texashistory.unt.edu/ark:/67531/metapth5868/: accessed March 14, 2012), University of North Texas Libraries, The Portal to Texas History, http://texashistory.unt.edu; crediting UNT Libraries, Denton, Texas.

4. David Binder, "'Hot Oil' Probe in Texas Called Bigger Than Billie Sol Estes Case," *Houston Chronicle*, July 15, 1962, sec. 1, p. 24.

5. Olen Clements, "$100,000 Oil Bribe Is Claimed," *Houston Chronicle*, July 15, 1962, p. 1.

6. Texas Legislature. House of Representatives. General Investigating Committee. *Official report to the House of Representatives of the 58th Legislature of Texas*, v. 1, 1963; digital images, (http://texashistory.unt.edu/ark:/67531/metapth5868/ : accessed March 14, 2012), University of North Texas Libraries, The Portal to Texas History, http://texashistory.unt.edu; crediting UNT Libraries, Denton, Texas.

7. Rangers Folder #29, Information Report (7/19/62) Ray to Crowder.

8. Rangers Folder # 30, Information Report (7/26/ 62) Ray to Crowder.

9. P. G. Lake funded H. L. Hunt's purchase of the Daisy Bradford well and surrounding acreage from Dad Joiner.

10. Rangers Folder #31, Information Report (8/2/62) Ray to Crowder.

11. Rangers Folder #33, Information Report (8/19/62) Ray to Crowder.

12. Thanks to Rusty Bloxom, Research Librarian at the Texas Rangers Museum and Library for identifying Ranger William Troy (Bud) Newberry in a telephone conversation of May 31, 2019. See also Chapter 17, Note 1. Ray had written only that Ranger Newberry had been present.

13. Rangers Folder # 36, Information Report (8/19/62), Ray to Crowder.

CHAPTER 20
THE HEARINGS

I noted in the Introduction that my first knowledge of the House General Investigating Committee and its plan to hold hearings came when my father received a tipoff call late on Saturday night, August 18, 1962. I met Ranger Glenn Elliott the next morning when he arrived at our home to serve my dad's subpoena. My parents and I went to Dallas on the following Sunday to be on hand for the first three-day session of the hearings that began on Monday morning.

Counsel for the committee, David Witts, began the hearing with a five-page opening statement, and then he called on Commission Chairman Bill Murray who noted that the first attempt to regulate directional drilling was in 1948—Murray's first year on the commission—when the commission adopted "statewide Rule No. 54 which required advance permission to drill a directional hole and after having completed it, required a verified directional survey by a third-party survey company sent directly to the commission." (1), (2)

Murray admitted he had received Ed Stanley's letter of April 19, 1950, in which Stanley warned the commission of unsubstantiated rumors of deviated wells. He also said, ". . .the Barber-Shell incident [in 1961] had jolted the RRC and they felt concern about wells that might have already been slanted."

Murray's only apparent attempt to control or stop slant drilling had been his rebuffed attempt to show AG Wilson his study of apparently slanted wells in January 1962. See Chapter 14.

Wilson testified after Murray and said, ". . .the slant well problem first came to his attention in April 1962 when he was first informed that Carter-Jones Drilling Company had drilled a well believed to be deviated." I guess he forgot Murray's request in January for an investigation. He sued Carter-Jones "seeking to cancel its charter and appoint a receiver to take over its books. The receiver went to Kilgore but the records had disappeared."

Assistant Attorney General David McAngus described in detail how commission engineer L. Dwight Murphy (sometimes known by his alias Robert V. Jobe) had received income amounting to nearly $150,000 in addition to his $7,000 annual salary between 1958 and 1962. The sources of this extra income included W. O. Davis who was the swindler in the Nortex Oil episode described in Chapter 18. Murphy also received an overriding royalty interest in the L. R. Jacobs lease on which Murphy had certified the #2 well as marginal and straight. See Chapter 18.

James Wendover of Nortex gave his view of the details of the "six-million-dollar swindle" already discussed in Chapter 18.

The star witness was Billy Joe James, also known as "Whipstock Bill," a noted expert at drilling directional wells who had worked in the East Texas Oil Field for 25 years.

James said that Ebro Oil, owned by W. O. Davis, hired him to set up the pipe connections and tank batteries on the Jacobs lease in October 1958. Using plastic pipe to prevent detection with a magnetic device, he installed an arrangement of pipes that allowed oil to be removed from the lease without having been passed through the tanks. Thus, oil could be stolen from the lease and sold as "hot oil"—oil produced illegally.

James told the committee he had worked on about 100 directional wells. He named Gibson Drilling, Carter-Jones, Crusader Oil, Stroud Brothers, and Ed Hearn, Sr. as some of the drilling contractors for whom he had drilled directional wells. He also said he knew of about 300 deviated wells in the East Texas Oil Field and that some whipstockers were so good "they can put it on a dime if you lay it out there 3,000 feet."

James described four ways by which a slanted well can be disguised:

1. Putting a pump jack on either a flowing well or a dummy well to make it look like a pumper;
2. Using trick photography; that is, running an exposed print from a straight well down a kicked well for the survey;
3. Drilling two holes side by side and running surveys down the straight hole;
4. Cutting a window in the casing of a straight well and kicking the well through the window

Assistant Attorney General Robert Flowers presented a long list of deposits into several bank accounts, eventually shown to be for the benefit of commission employee Nelson Decker, totaling about $47,000 in addition to his monthly salary of $430. After Ranger Ray described his discussions with Decker, discussed in Chapter 17, Decker refused to testify, citing Fifth Amendment rights.

Of the remaining six suspected deviators scheduled to testify, all but Judge David Moore refused to testify. Moore's testimony was just obfuscation and "I just can't recall."

Finally, committee counsel Witts summed up by noting that "at lease 124 wells had been found to be deviated" in excess of the permissible three degrees. He estimated that 350 deviated wells would eventually be found in the East Texas field, and that slanted wells in other fields would appear as investigations progressed. Among the deviated wells found thus far, some had been deviated by as much as 60 degrees from vertical, and extended more than a half-mile horizontally. He noted that in such an extensive enterprise, the practice of deviation must have been widely known and without action by local or state officials, and that collusion by commission personnel with the deviators was obvious.

With that summary by Witts, the committee adjourned to reconvene again in Dallas on September 10.

On September 8, Ranger Ray reported that 143 deviated wells had been discovered in the East Texas, Hawkins, and Quitman fields. These wells, according to informants, amount to about one-third of the total number of crooked wells. (3)

The second session was more dramatic than the first. Among the first 22 men called, including my father, all refused to testify save the first, J. L. Gulley, who said that he owned interests in some deviated wells, but was unaware of their being deviated.

Witness number 23 was Harry M. Harrington Jr. (4) According to Witts, Harrington "testified volubly." Harrington admitted owning interests in a number of deviated wells, but insisted that he knew nothing of their being deviated. He did admit that the attorney general, Humble, and Texaco sued him demanding "approximately 15 million dollars" for theft of oil. He denied ever having discussed the merits of these suits with his partners. He stated: "financial institutions in Dallas had lost over 25 million dollars on these oil loans and that, therefore, the legislature should pass laws to protect lenders so that 90 days after a well was drilled and no contest filed by an offset [adjoining] owner, then that lease and all activities on it should be closed from inspection."

Harrington, an Eagle Scout and a lawyer, had the chutzpah to state that he did not believe it a violation of law to produce oil from a lease belonging to another person or company without consent! Of course, the Rule of Capture allows one to produce oil that migrates into his legal wellbore, but not intentional theft.

Harrington said the only slanted well about which he had any knowledge was Humble Oil's Roy Laird well in the Hawkins field, but a commission survey showed this well to have a maximum inclination of 2 ½ degrees near the bottom of the well.

He continued with an attack on the East Texas Salt Water Disposal Company and its reinjection of produced salt water back into the East Texas field since 1942. Witts told Harrington that the "Salt Water Company" would be dealt with in a future hearing.

After another eight suspected deviators refused to testify, Pleas Dawson provided some comic relief. Dawson said, "... he worked for an oil company in 1952 and quit just before he got fired." But now he owned some 300 wells in the State of Texas, 105 of them in the East Texas field. Of his 300 wells, Dawson said he operated 73. Witts asked, "Well, that is a remarkable success story. Can you tell us how you went about acquiring some 300 producing wells since 1952?" Dawson replied, "Well, sir, I would be scared to let the trade secret out here publicly. I really would. I don't think I am smart." Committeeman DeWitt Hale asked Dawson whether he might divulge his secret in a private session. (5)

Gregg County Commissioner Jack Bean, who had served in that office for 18 years, testified that he knew that Judge Earl Sharp had been subpoenaed to testify at the first hearing in Dallas, August 27, 28, and 29, and that Sharp had attended a commissioners meeting on August 30. Bean said he owned a one-thirty-second interest in Sharp's T. P. Coal and Oil Lease for which he had paid $2,000 in 1958, and that this interest had provided $2,000 per year income ever since. He never discussed the plugging of this well with Sharp. He said further that the Commissioners Court on September 10 granted Sharp permission to leave the state on September 8. Bean said that he possibly would have given Sharp permission to leave the state to avoid his subpoena, because Sharp had been ill and was having blackouts during the past two or three months. Bean also said he had contributed $5,000 to Sharp's settlement with Texaco. (6)

Gregg Commissioner John Allen said that both the county and the district judges had been missing from Gregg County, but he knew nothing.

Except for Harrington's performance, the second session of HGIC hearings closed with little to report.

On September 13, Jim Ray submitted, at the request of Col. Garrison, a set of recommendations for the prevention, detection, and correction of such activities as those now exposed in East Texas. Ray's suggestions can be summarized as: (1.) Establish impartial laws, rules, and regulations that do not favor any party over another; (2.) Require all new wells to be demonstrated legal with witnessed surveys, logs, and pipe tallies; (3.) Eliminate or modify the Marginal Well Rule to eliminate incentive for cheating; (4.) Require complete history of all oil leases; (5.) Set up special crews at the Railroad Commission with authority to investigate any well within the state at will; (6.) Make operators of adjacent leases responsible for detecting and reporting violations; and (7.) Change or eliminate "curve-out wells." (7)

On September 14, 1962, a federal grand jury seated in Tyler returned the first criminal indictments in the slant-hole affair: 109 indictments against brothers J. D. and W. V. Stroud of Henderson. Charges included transporting 14,000 barrels of hot oil (oil produced in violation of one or more regulations) and for making false statements to the Federal Petroleum Board concerning such transport. (8)

The committee convened again on September 25 in Houston where the first item of business was discussion of the J. W. Tyner Trust, into which interests in numerous deviated wells had been held for the benefit of L. D. Murphy and Nelson Decker. Murphy's interests appeared under his alias Robert. V. Jobe. Deviators who had contributed to the Tyner Trust from their deviated wells included: Amtex Oil, E. M. Fisk, T. F. Patton, Robert Cargill, Earl Sharp, and E. W. (Jelly) Scates. Of the $150,000 deposited into the Tyner Trust, about $50,000 came from Scates.

The committee called on J. W. Tyner who asked that the committee be questioned "without the benefit of the oath." Chairman Hollowell declined and Tyner was sworn, but he refused to answer any questions citing attorney-client confidentiality. AG Wilson told Tyner that the invocation of privilege in an illegal transaction "is in effect bribery" and that in such a case, he would pursue the matter with the State Bar Grievance Committee.

Hugh Camp, another Gregg County Commissioner who'd served for 18 years, acknowledged owning interests in slanted wells operated by Tom Cook Jr. and Earl Sharp. Assistant Attorney General Robert Flowers then revealed that Hearn Directional Drilling Company, Kern Directional Drilling Company, and Drilling Control, a Louisiana company, and William Hobbs Directional Drilling Company had filed false directional surveys on deviated wells with the Railroad Commission. But when M. X. Hobbs was called to testify, he refused.

After former commission engineer Ed Stanley refused to testify, the committee called on William Joseph Hamby of Schlumberger. He couldn't explain why a survey on Mark Oil's M. C. Elliott #3 well that bore his signature showed an inclination of 1.75 degrees at 3,500 feet total depth, while an Eastman survey of the same well showed a deviation of 53 degrees and a total depth of 5,071 feet. Phil Gaines, who at the time worked for Schlumberger, had similar lack of understanding when his survey of Mark Oil's Culver #3 and that run by Eastman had equally differing results. David Cowart another Schlumberger employee, came accompanied by Schlumberger's general counsel. He gave a lecture on directional surveys, and claimed that six surveys run by the company "accurately represented the condition of these holes at the time these surveys were run."

Perry Blanton, Chairman of the Federal Petroleum Board, appeared accompanied by Richard Allerman, an attorney with the Department of the Interior. Allermam advised the committee and AG Wilson that employees of the department had been instructed "not to discuss any matters relating to the functions of the federal government."

Four more deviators refused to testify before Frank Briscoe, District Attorney for Harris County, said that he was preparing to submit the matter of a deviated well in the Webster-Friendswood field not far southeast of Houston to the Harris County Grand Jury. With Briscoe's brief testimony, the committee adjourned until September 27 when it would reconvene in Austin.

The committee opened its Austin session with Witts reviewing Harrington's attacks on the East Texas Salt Water Disposal Company. In particular, Harrington asserted that the company's reinjection of produced salt water into the western side of the field caused oil within the Woodbine to move eastward. He claimed such movement deprived the west-side mineral and lease owners to lose their rightful owners farther east. He admitted that the west-side owners had been compensated through the application of curve-outs. None of the facts diminished Harrington's attack on the Salt Water Company. (9)

Bryan W. Payne, an independent operator who had been president of the Salt Water Company since its inception in 1942, testified in rebuttal to Harrington's assertion that reinjection of produced water pushed oil away from its original place. He said, "It is a physical impossibility to do any pushing of the oil, or anything else. Anybody knows that knows what the Woodbine Sand is, it is a heavy sand, and lots of them would call it a rock. For the uninitiated, it is a rock-type sand, and you can't push anything through it."

W. S. Morris, vice president and general manager of the company (and also a professional engineer), spoke of the company's business with somewhat greater clarity. But he still denied that fluids could move within the Woodbine sand. Were that a true statement, oil could not flow into the wellbores. How could a single oil well produce more than 100,000 barrels of oil during its life time unless oil flowed into the wellbore through and from the Woodbine Sandstone?

In fact, the reinjected salt water replaces oil and water removed from the reservoir and decreases the rate at which the reservoir pressure decreases with oil (and salt water) production. Thus, the reinjection extends the life of the field and allows more oil to be removed from the rock that Payne and Morris insisted was impermeable.

Representatives of 14 major oil companies testified that none of their companies had drilled any unauthorized deviated wells. Then Richard Alleman, representing Dan Purvis, a former chairman of the Federal Petroleum Board, noted that Purvis had met in the attorney general's office with AG Wilson, but he provided no information to the committee. Commissioner and former lieutenant governor Ben Ramsey, who had been appointed to the commission when Olin Culberson died in 1961, had nothing to say. Bill Murray closed the hearing by denying again that he had knowledge of the slant-hole activity earlier than1960, not mentioning the Ed Stanley letter of April 19, 1950.

The committee scheduled its final session for October 29, 1962.

NOTES

1. The HGIC Report of 93 pages reviews five hearings held by the House General Investigating Committee between August 27 and October 29, 1962, composed by committee counsel David A. Witts. I have provided in the Notes for Chapter 19 the official citation for the Report.

2. The HGIC comprised Charles Ballman, chairman; Bill Hollowell, vice chairman; Menton Murray; DeWitt Hale; and W. H. Pieratt.

3. Rangers Folder # 41, Information Report, (9/8/62), Ray to Crowder.

4. I noted in Chapter 7 that Harrington was among the cabal that drilled the first deviated wells in East Texas, and in Chapter 9, Harrington was master of ceremonies for the dedication of the Boy Scout well.

5. This is the same Pleas Dawson who had come to a satisfactory understanding with Captain Bob Crowder in August. See Chapter 19.

6. The Texaco Lease was presumably adjacent to Sharp's T. P Coal and Oil Lease. I have no documentation of Sharp's settlement.

7. I have not mentioned curve-out wells in this book. When a well's production has ceased to be profitable, primarily because of the volume of salt water produced along with decreasing volumes of oil and the expense of disposal of the water, one can plot a curve from which he can project the total volume of oil the well could produce in the future. That volume can be added to the allowable of a more productive well if the transferring well is abandoned. The operator of such wells can then produce the "curve-out allowable" from the receiving well. The curve-outs were often abused by commission personnel and by cheating operators.

8. Fred Pass, "2 East Texans Indicted on Oil Piracy Charges," *The Dallas Morning News*, September 15, 1962, p. 1.

9. See "Shakeup in Oil Regulations Urged at Hearing," *Longview Daily News*,
    September 12, 1962, gives a more detailed summary of Harrington's
    testimony than does the committee's report.

CHAPTER 21
THE SALT-WATER COMPANY

Despite the testimony of the witnesses in Austin, my research into the East Texas Salt Water Disposal Company provides for a somewhat different account of events regarding the operation of the company.

As production of oil progressed, many wells, especially those drilled deep into the Woodbine sand and those on the western side of the field, began to produce increasing volumes of salty water along with oil. At first, the salty water so produced was allowed to run onto the ground and into creeks and the Sabine River. This pollution had to be stopped, and reinjection of produced water might be a solution.

The first salt water disposal well went into operation in June 1938. Through it, 224,000 barrels of produced salt water went back into the Woodbine reservoir. The next year, the state brought an injunction against operators to prevent pollution of the Neches-Angelina watershed, and the operators were forced to act. (1)

On July 29, 1941, Joe Zeppa, an independent operator from Tyler who founded Delta Drilling Company, proposed to the Railroad Commission that he be allowed to drill an injection well into which he would dispose of salt water produced by others. He further proposed that owners of wells who returned all the produced salt water from their wells be given an additional one-barrel-per-day oil allowable for each source well.

The Secretary of State of Texas approved the charter of a new corporation, the East Texas Salt Water Disposal Company, Inc., on January 20, 1942, for the purpose:

"To gather and impound water containing salt or other substance produced in the drilling and operation of oil wells and other wells and to prevent the flow of such water into streams at times when such streams may be used for irrigation, and to have and exercise all of the functions and powers authorized by the laws of Texas, and particularly by Chapters XVI, of Title 32, and Articles 7572, 7573, and 7574 of the Revised Civil Statutes of Texas, 1925, and all amendments thereto."

Within eight days of its formation, the company authorized an increase in its capital stock from $25,000 to $2 million and specifically stated that it would serve all operators in the field without discrimination and would give no preferred treatment to stockholders or any other person, group, or company.

By 1958, when the company's second report appeared, and from which I have taken this information, the company had disposed of more than 1.7 million barrels of produced salt water at an average cost to the operators of less than 1.5 cents per barrel. In addition to the cost-effective disposal of the produced brine, this replacement of produced water has been a key factor in the maintenance of adequate reservoir pressure such that the ultimate recovery of oil in place will be about 80 percent, a phenomenal recovery factor. (2)

Joe Zeppa deserves a special star in his crown for devising the Salt Water Company, as it is now often called.

Some have argued that the reinjection of produced water resulted in an increased rate at which the new western production limit would move eastward and thereby deprive both royalty owners and operators on the western side of the field of their rightful income. Harry Harrington vigorously advanced this argument. Clearly, he was correct, Payne and Morris notwithstanding. And there are some cases in which one operator intentionally injected produced salt water to flood out a neighboring operator in retaliation for some real or perceived offense. In one case of which I have personal knowledge, the victim operator was a friend of mine.

A further argument could be made (and was made by some) that the original oil in place was greater on the western side than on the eastern side because the Woodbine sand is much thicker toward the west. Thus it is arguably unfair that the owners of east-side wells should continue to produce oil in 2019 while west-side interests had been abandoned in the

1940s. For many—Harrington among them—the claimed acceleration of west-side abandonment created animosity toward the Salt Water Disposal Company. The East Texas Field was just too big, and there were too many operators by the time the extent of the field was known, to allow a reasonable unitization of the field and allow equitable sharing of the bounty.

I have already described how the column of salty water, which provides the driving pressure for the reservoir, moves upward and eastward as oil is removed from the Black Giant. When wells began to produce water along with oil, something had to be done with the water. Joe Zeppa's company was the answer.

Clearly, the reinjection of produced water helps to maintain the pressure within the reservoir; but in the vicinity of an injection well, the local pressure is increased by a significant amount. This increased pressure from the injected water is capable of pushing nearby oil away from its original location. Harrington was correct in his assertion that injection wells could be used to manipulate the location of oil within the Woodbine reservoir.

Payne and Morris should have known their testimony was inconsistent with elementary physics; after all, they were professional oil producers. Even the committee members, none members of the oil producing fraternity, should have seen through Payne and Morris's testimony. As evidenced by their testimony in Austin, Payne and Morris clearly did not understand the mechanics of the flow of oil through the Woodbine sand. They swore that oil could not flow through the rock.

If oil and water can't flow through the Woodbine sand, as claimed by Payne and Morris, production of oil would be impossible. I cannot understand why the committee failed to recognize this fault in the Payne and Morris testimony unless they were already committed to a chosen outcome irrespective of the fundamental physics of reservoir engineering. AG Wilson, a geologist by training, certainly knew that Payne and Morris were incorrect, but even he didn't comment on it. This leaves me unable to avoid the conclusion that in his zeal to convict the deviators—Harrington, in particular—the attorney general was willing to allow the erroneous testimony to stand unchallenged.

Although the subject of the reinjection of produced water was hotly debated, it amounted to a side issue at the hearing. The ETSWDC remains one of the best plans ever devised within the oil industry, and Harrington's performance at the hearing did nothing to enhance his reputation other than as a blowhard.

In 2012, the National Research Council issued a paper in which the Council considered the reinjection of recovered frack water and produced water a potential cause of minor earthquakes. (3) The ETSWDC has been reinjecting produced water back into the Woodbine for almost 90 years without a hint of earthquakes.

NOTES

1. The Angelina and Neches Rivers run more or less parallel to the Sabine River and join between the small towns of Jasper and Woodville. The resulting Neches flows into the Sabine at Port Neches just above the Gulf of Mexico.

2. Staff, East Texas Salt Water Disposal Company, *Salt Water Disposal, East Texas Oil Field*, 2nd ed., Petroleum Extension Service, University of Texas Extension Service, Austin, TX, 1958.

3. National Research Council. "Executive Summary." Induced Seismicity in Energy Technologies, National Academies Press, Washington, DC, 2012.

In the month between the fourth and fifth meetings of the investigating committee, all was not quiet.

Nortex sued Ebro in Dallas County District Court on September 20, 1962, claiming fraud. The jury "found special issues in favor of Ebro and against Nortex," but the court granted a motion for retrial, and, "based on a stipulation, entered a judgment for Nortex against Ebro in the sum of $3,903,000." Note that both Ebro and Elba companies had already been dissolved by Davis. Nonetheless, Ebro and Elba seem to have been used interchangeably by newspapers and investigators. (1), (2)

Ranger Ray remained busy. The Rusk County grand jury was scheduled to meet on October 3, and the Gregg County grand jury would meet on twelve days later, to consider indictments in the slant-hole matter. Col. Garrison had instructed Rangers to be available to the district attorneys of these two counties as well as of Upshur and Wood counties. Ott Duncan of Upshur County was the most eager of the DAs to deal with the matter and move on. Ray and Read reviewed evidence of activities in Upshur County with Duncan on September 27 and 28. And on October 2, . Ray brought two assistant attorneys general, David McAngus and Frank Maloney, as well as DPS agents Bill Kavanaugh and George Read to help encourage Duncan. The Upshur grand jury had no trouble indicting 12 men on a total of 15 counts on the following day. Those indicted included Robert Matthews and L. Dwight Murphy, a Tyler attorney, and nine deviators. (3)

The same group of lawmen plus AG Wilson assembled on the fourth of October to review evidence with Gregg County DA Ralph Prince. That night, Ray received a phone call in which the caller told Ray that deviator defense counsel Fred Erisman had met with Duncan just an hour after the lawmen had departed. The caller said six members of the Gregg grand jury were related to or controlled by deviators, and that the foreman was a close personal friend of accused Judge David Moore. (4)

On October 8, Bill Kavanaugh reported that deviated wells had been drilled in Ector, Jackson, and Victoria counties, as well as in East Texas. (5) By November, deviated wells had been discovered in the Freindswood-Webster field in Harris County, the Ganado field in Jackson County, the Hopson field in Karnes County, the Coke and Quitman fields in Wood County, and the Danville field in Rusk County. The slant-hole activity had spread significantly. (6)

Ray reported to Capt. Crowder that his two informants had said that "Bill Murray has been involved with the crooked hole operators all along," and "had been receiving money from them through a Christian Youth Organization that Murray heads. The operators were said to have purchased a building and lot in Austin and spent thousands of dollars remodeling this building into a boys dormitory." Ray then revealed that these informants had said in May that R. S. Medley, a deviator, had told one of them that Earl Sharp had sent letters to all the deviators inviting them to a dinner at the Longview Hotel in honor of Bill Murray to raise $20,000 for Murray's Christian organization. Sharp was most unhappy when only a few of those invited attended. Sharp called the absentees the next day to express his disappointment. Ray included in this report of October 16, that Stanley McCubbin, a deviator, had told the informants that the deviators had had a mole in the attorney general's office who kept the deviators informed of Wilson's moves. McCubbin's statement confirms my assertion in the Introduction that a mole had tipped off those deviators to whom subpoenas were to be served in August. (7) One must be careful when evaluating reports from confidential informants.

The Gregg County grand jury filed 71 indictments against 17 men on October 17. These included 10 counts against Nelson Decker, 15 against L. D. Murphy, nine against J. W. Tyner, and 13 against G. U. Yoachum, two against B. J. Hallmark of Schlumberger, and the remaining 22 against 12 deviators. (8)

NOTES

1. See Chapter 18 and Chapter 13.

2. "Nortex Files 5-Million Suit," *The Dallas Morning News*, September 21, 1962, p. 1.

3. I have listed all indictments along with charges from each of the four county grand juries in the Appendix.

4. Rangers Folder # 45, Interoffice Memorandum (10/7/62) Ray to Crowder.

5. Rangers Folder # 47, (10/8/62) Kavanaugh to Garrison.

6. Dawson Duncan, "Eight Fields Now Involved in Slant-Hole Scandal," *The Dallas Morning News*, November 17, 1962, p. 7.

7. Rangers Folder # 49, Interoffice Memorandum (10/16/62) Ray to Crowder.

8. Rangers Folder # 52, Interoffice Memorandum (11/3/62) Ray to Crowder.

The last of the five hearings of the HGIC convened on October 29 in Dallas, but neither Judge Earl Sharp nor Judge David Moore, both under subpoena, was present. Fred Erisman presented a doctor's statement for Judge Sharp, and Moore was reported to be in trial of a capital case in Austin.

James R. Lewis was the first witness. He had served on the Federal Petroleum Board for 18 years until the end of November 1953, and as its chair beginning in 1948. He told the committee that the board's first action regarding slanted wells began in late 1952 in the Delhi field in Louisiana, and that a general investigation of directional drilling began around March 1953. That summer, a special investigator from the Secretary of the Interior's office appeared from Washington. (1) Lewis told of the investigator's hostility toward his investigations. He also told that the two argued bitterly after office hours. The investigator insisted that the subject was strictly a state matter and that Lewis should cease his investigation immediately. Lewis rebutted that a violation of the (federal) "Connally Hot Oil Act of 1935" was a federal matter.

In a memorandum dated June 23, 1953, Lewis stated that two civil suits had been filed in the 114th District Court of Smith County in Tyler in 1954 after the discovery of deviated wells, one suit naming Blaine Dunbar and the second naming Reid Allgood as defendants. Allgood filed a Plea of Privilege and got the case transferred to Judge David Moore's court in Gregg County. Lewis asked Judge Sharp for help in finding local counsel for the prosecution. He said that Judge Sharp was cordial and tried to help, but he was unable to hire satisfactory local counsel in Gregg County. Moore granted Allgood a Summary Judgment. Lewis appealed to the Sixth Court of Appeals in Texarkana, and while the appeal was pending, the litigants reached a settlement in the Tyler court.

Asked whether he suspected that any Railroad Commission personnel had been bribed, Lewis responded, "I always had occasion to believe that, General Wilson. I was—I was the instigator in two or three different prosecutions where Railroad Commission members went to the penitentiary." (2), (3)

Nelson Puett, another twenty-year veteran of the Federal Petroleum Board, and its chair from 1955 to 1960 did not trust the Railroad Commission. In his view, anything the commission learned about a Petroleum Board investigation would go immediately to the accused operator. "He pointed to the lawsuits and fines that had been tried and paid, all of which were matters of public record, dating back as far as 1953." But neither Murray nor Wilson had known of them. Or so they said.

Puett noted that he and one of his agents had gauged a well as producing one to two barrels of oil per day; and shortly thereafter Nelson Decker gauged the same well at eight barrels per day (about 2,500 barrels per year). That fake eight-barrel daily allowable, apparently transferred to another well, would have been valuable to someone.

DPS agent George Reed confirmed he had demonstrated that Robert V. Jobe was an alias used by L. D. Murphy. After Reed affirmed his recollection of Judge Moore's denying that he knew Robert V. Jobe, counsel presented him a check signed by David C. Moore, payable to Robert V. Jobe, and deposited to the J. W. Tyner Trustee Account. Judge Moore's credibility suffered. (4)

As the session closed, Attorney General Wilson said, "I can think of at least three counties in Texas where the honesty of public officials is far below any acceptable standard, and I do not see a sign of any majority of the people in those counties really willing to correct the situation."

The Wood County Grand Jury kicked off November by indicting 14 individuals on a total of 35 counts. Attorney General Wilson had personally attended the grand jury session and had questioned at least some of the accused. Among those called before the grand jury was Robert Allgood, then the 22-year-old son of Reid Allgood.

Robert had just been graduated from SMU and had begun his first job as a federal bank examiner when the Wood County Grand Jury subpoenaed him for testimony. Wilson grilled Robert before the grand jurors. He presented documents bearing Robert's "signature" that had been notarized by Harry Harrington, and demanded to know whether these were Robert's signatures. Robert responded that the dates on the documents showed that he was a boy of eight to 10 years at the time, and not only had he had not signed them, he knew nothing of the slant-hole activity at the time. Nonetheless, at Wilson's urging, the grand jury indicted Robert. Interestingly, Robert's name does not appear in the Wood County Grand Jury's list of indictments from either of its two sessions; but he does appear as a defendant in one of 14 penalty suits filed against 27 individuals and Carter-Jones Drilling Company on April 4, 1963, by the new attorney general. Gene Matthews, a personal friend of the Allgoods and president of the First National Bank in Longview, had asked AG Wilson to dismiss Robert's indictment. Wilson refused. (5)

The grand jury indicted Judge Sharp for bribery and theft, L. D. Murphy for accepting a bribe, and J. W. Tyner for being an accomplice to theft; the remaining counts were conspiracy to commit theft and/or theft. (6) Then, on November 9, the Rusk County Grand Jury issued indictments against 18 individuals on a total of 37 counts, all of which were theft and/or conspiracy to commit theft. (7)

During the last two weeks of November, a survey crew encountered resistance from suspected deviator Pete Davis when they attempted to run a survey on his J. B. Webb wells in Upshur County, but an injunction from AG Wilson dissolved Davis's resistance. At about the same time, Pleas Dawson, recalling his earlier encounter with an irate Bob Crowder, offered no resistance to the surveying of his wells, "almost all" of which proved to be deviated.

The big news came on December 11 when a "Blue Ribbon" Grand Jury in Gregg County filed 209 indictments against 44 men. Each of Rex Stegall, A. E. (Jack) McCubbin, W. T. Maxwell, J. K. Maxwell, was charged with 22 counts. The remaining 40 men were charged with the other 121 counts. Judge David Moore and Judge Earl Sharp were among the 40. Moore quickly demanded an immediate trial, telling the Associated Press, "I believe I can establish my innocence when all the facts are presented to a jury." (8)

Even with the indictments already noted, Ray was concerned that none of the district attorneys was eager to pursue indictments in the slant-hole matter. None wanted to go to trial, fearing that local jurors would never convict their neighbors on charges of stealing oil from Big Oil. (9)

Meanwhile, in Tyler, a new sheriff had come to town. William Wayne Justice had taken office as U. S. Attorney for the Eastern District of Texas on July 1, 1961, a Kennedy appointee. Late in 1962, the aptly-named Justice got the Justice Department's approval to seek federal indictments against at least one group of deviators for violating the 1935 Connolly Hot Oil Act—shipping illegally-produced oil in interstate commerce. Federal Judge Joe Sheehy, was not keen on having the federal government involved in what he saw as a state issue. "It was rumored around the courthouse that a number of wealthy Tyler oil people with whom Sheehy socialized had been involved in slant oil activities and were prevailing upon him to discourage the prosecution." But a federal grand jury granted Justice and his partner Leighton Cornett indictments against several groups. Among those indicted on 29 counts were Daryl Gaumer, E. B. Hearn Sr., E. B. Hearn Jr., and Associates Drilling Company, a company owned by Gaumer and Hearn. (10), (11), (12), (13)

NOTES

1. Lewis said the investigator's name was Mr. Hupingjams. I was unable to find a Mr. Hupingjams in a brief Google search.

2. I could not find a case of a commissioner or a commission employee who had been sent to prison. But employees who tried to enforce the rules have been fired. (3)

3. Fred Hasemeyer, "Fired: Texas Regulators Say They Tried to Enforce Rules, Lost Jobs," *InsideClimate News*, December 9, 2014, https://publicintegrity.org/environment/fired-texas-regulators-say-they-tried-to-enforce-rules-lost-jobs/

4. Ed Cocke, "Oil Quiz: One Mum and Three Missing," *The Dallas Morning News*, October 30, 1962, p. 1.

5. Personal interviews with Robert Allgood.

6. See Chapter 7, Note 2.

7. Rangers Folder # 52, Interoffice Memorandum (11/3/62) Ray to Crowder.

8. Rangers Folder # 53, Interoffice Memorandum (11/11/62) Ray to Crowder.

9. "209 Counts in Oil Study," *Fort Worth Star-Telegram*, December 12, 1962, pp. 1 and 5.

10. Rangers Folder # 57, Interoffice Memorandum (12/13/62) Ray to Crowder.

11. Frank R. Kemerer, *William Wayne Justice, A Judicial Biography*, University of Texas Press, Austin, TX, 1991, pp. 50-55.

12. "Jury Picked For trial of 3 Oilmen," *The Dallas Morning News*, June 4, 1963, p. 4.

13. William Wayne Justice was promoted to the bench of the Eastern Federal District of Texas in 1968, where he served with vigor until he retired (took senior status) on June 30, 1998. He continued to serve in the latter capacity until his death on October 13, 2009. The retired Judge Justice and his elegant wife Sue often attended the Presidential Lecture Series at the University of Texas at Tyler in the 1990s, as did I. We came to know each other as friends. The judge was not very popular in conservative East Texas, but I came to love and respect him highly. I heard him speak to Rotarians once when he said, "I know most of you don't like many of my rulings; but governments change. And when you are no longer the majority, you'll be thankful for my rulings." How true that is today!

CHAPTER 24
1963

The new year had hardly begun when the investigating committee's chairman, Bill Hollowell, filed a contempt of the legislature citation against Earl Sharp, the former Gregg County Judge who had resigned on November 12. (1)

On January 15, 1963, Will Wilson surrendered the office of Texas Attorney General, to Waggoner Carr, a former two-term Speaker of the Texas House of Representatives and a Wilson rival. On the same day, John C. Connally became governor. After leaving office in January 1963, Wilson established his own law firm and brought in some major clients, most notably, Humble Oil. This arrangement convinced many in East Texas, especially the deviators, that Wilson had acted as Humble's stooge during the Slant-Hole affair. (2)

Carr was at a disadvantage when he assumed Wilson's old office because his rival and predecessor failed to pass on to him the knowledge he had gained during his slant-hole investigation. Nonetheless, the Wood County Grand Jury brought indictments against seven men on 18 counts on February 6. With these indictments, the grand juries of Gregg, Rusk, Upshur, and Wood Counties indicted a total of 63 individuals on a total of 392 criminal counts. Wilson had filed civil penalty suits against almost 100 accused deviators in Travis County District Court seeking a total of $25.5 million before he left office, and new attorney general Carr filed similar penalty suits against 79 individuals. These suits called for penalties of $1,000 per day of illegal production for wells operated for more than 30 days. (3), (4), (5)

After the Investigating Committee completed its public hearings— five sessions between August 27, 1962, and October 29, 1962—the committee's general counsel David Witts recounted the changes brought about by the hearings in the committee's published report to the Legislature in early 1963. (6)

The committee's official report, written after the hearings had closed, opens on page one with these words followed by four pages summarizing events prior to the hearing, written by Witts:

"It will probably go down in history as the seven days that changed the face of the Texas oil and gas industry. Although the investigation centered in East Texas, the findings and results of those seven days of public hearings have state wide and even national significance."

The report goes on. "In the wake of the hearings have come indictments, procedural changes of the RRC, improvements of conservation practices and stronger and healthier oil and gas industry," wrote Witts.

But this statement was largely posturing on Witts' part. He was implying that the federal and state indictments against 74 individuals arose from the hearings, but these would probably have been handed down with or without the hearings. Likewise, the 57 civil penalty suits filed by Attorney General Wilson against 67 individuals and nine companies would probably have been filed based on the investigations of the Texas Rangers without any help from the hearings. These suits seeking $25 million in penalties for slant-hole activities resulted in judgments, but only a small fraction of the money was ever collected. (7), (8)

The Railroad Commission had proposed revisions of its rules on August 16, before the hearings had even begun, and in late September, the commission announced that new rules regarding spacing of wells would be effective October 1. New rules doubled from 20 to 40 acres the statewide minimum acreage for a full allowable well, and the minimum distance from a lease line rose from 330 feet to 467 feet. In the East Texas Oil Field, however, the rules adopted in 1944 allowed one well per five acres, and in cases where an owner had a smaller tract, a full allowable well could be permitted. The new 40-acre spacing had no effect on East Texas, where the minimum acreage for a new well remained five acres. The commission could not undo the drilling of more than 20,000 wells, most of which had been drilled on five-acre spacing or on smaller tracts.

The commission also required a directional survey on any well that deviated by five degrees or more, with the location of the bottom of the hole identified, a rule that was upheld in a district court on December

14. But nobody would volunteer that his well deviates in excess of the five degrees if he intended to steal oil from an adjoining lease.

The commission announced a more effective rule change in December 1962. The new rule outlawed the Tom Thumb Pump (a miniature pump guaranteed not to bring more than 20 barrels per day) and the East Texas Choke (a device that guaranteed a production of exactly 19 barrels per day.) Deviators and the majors who drilled slanted holes used both of these devices so as to have them classified as marginal. Now, all wells classified as marginal would undergo annual tests witnessed by commission personnel, but Murray acknowledged that even these steps would have little effect on operators determined to circumvent the rules. The House committee did recommend that the Legislature pass a statute that would eliminate the incentive to classify a well as marginal.

The 58th Legislature finished its biennial 140-day session at the end of May 1963. One newspaper reported, "The Legislature spurned every effort to write stronger laws against slant-hole drilling at this session. And it gave like treatment to another controversy—small-tract drilling—which loomed high on the pre-session agenda." So much for the effectiveness of the committee's hearings. (9)

One new statute related to the scandal was passed by the Legislature. In response to Wilson's collecting monies from major oil companies to fund his investigations (which was legal at the time), Rep. Ben Barnes, later lieutenant governor, proposed and guided through the Legislature a bill that prohibited the attorney general's accepting donations for investigations or trials of lawsuits. Although Governor Connally had not signed the bill into law at the time of the committee's report, there is no indication of a pocket veto. Current state law—Texas Statutes, Section 402.005—does prohibit the attorney general from accepting money offered by an individual, firm, partnership, corporation, or association for investigating or prosecuting a matter.

Ten bills died after having been introduced. Rep. George Hinson proposed allowing lawsuits concerning violation of commission rules to be defended in the county in which the alleged violation occurred. It failed, and jurisdiction for such lawsuits remained in Travis County (Austin).

Rep. Ronald Roberts' bill to license surveyors who make directional surveys of wells died in a House committee. Sen. William Moore wanted to provide for adjustment of oil ownership when settlements are made for alleged drainage via slanted wells, but his bill suffered a similar fate in committee. Rep. Emmett Lack and Rep. Clyde Haynes Jr. proposed increasing the Railroad Commission from three to five members, a proposal that also died in committee.

Bill Hollowell and Menton Murray, the two members of the committee who were not retiring, asked to make "theft of oil" through deviated drilling a specific criminal offense. Their bill passed in the House but died in a Senate committee. Hollowell introduced a second bill, which would make reports and statements to the Railroad Commission subject to perjury penalties, died in a House committee.

Bob Eckhardt's bill to revise conflict of interest laws and the state's Code of Ethics passed the House, but it died in a Senate committee. A second bill authorizing the Railroad Commission to require pooling of small tracts into larger drilling units if voluntary efforts to do so failed also died in the House.

The Legislature failed to enact any significant laws that might curtail the drilling of crooked wells because no powerful interests pushed such reform. Three members of the House General Investigating Committee—Charles Ballman, DeWitt Hale, and W. H. Pieratt—had retired from the Legislature at the close of the 1962 session. Attorney General Will Wilson left office in January 1963, and was succeeded by Waggoner Carr. These absences, along with the public's unfavorable opinion of Big Oil and the continuing influence of independent oilmen—with their personal relationships and their campaign contributions—all contributed to the absence of legislative action. Witts' claim of an effective series of hearings was wishful thinking or revisionist history.

Attorney General Carr filed a motion to dismiss the indictment against young Robert Allgood because "he personally took no part in any manner in the acts complained of, the same taking place without his knowledge or consent." Austin Judge Herman Jones granted the motion to dismiss on May 29, 1963. During my research for this book in the district clerk's office in Austin, I found Robert's dismissal. I gave my copy of the document to Robert when we met on December 16, 2006.

The case against Hearn Sr., Hearn Jr., Gaumer, and their company went to trial on June 3, 1963 before an antagonistic Judge Sheehy, who granted defendants' motion to dismiss all the felony counts, leaving 17 misdemeanor counts against Gaumer and Hearn Jr., and Associates Drilling Company. (10) The jury convicted Hearn Jr. of conspiracy, and Associates on 14 counts of filing false reports. Sheehy dismissed all counts against Hearn Sr. (11) On September 3, Sheehy sentenced Gaumer to $250 fines and six months on each of counts. He fined Hearn Jr. $2,000 and six months, suspended for a year. And Associates was fined $250 on each of 14 counts. All of these fines to be "collected on execution only." This means that defendants are not sent to jail for unpaid fines. (12)

NOTES

1. "Ex-Judge Cited for Contempt," *Fort Worth Star-Telegram*, January 8, 1963, sec. 1, p. 2.

2. I heard my father and his cronies accuse Wilson of having been in bed with Humble when I was in Longview for brief visits in 1963 and 1964.

3. Austin Bureau of The News, "14 Slant Oil Penalty Suits Filed by State," *The Dallas Morning News*, April 5, 1963, sec. 1, p. 5.

4. "Eight More Suits Filed," *Fort Worth Star-Telegram*, May 30, 1963, sec. 3, p. 5.

5. Ronnie Dugger, "Attorney General Discusses: The Oil Survey Fund," *The Texas Observer*, July 27, 1962, pp. 1, 4.

6. See Chapter 20 Note 1.

7. "Bills to Get Top Priority," *Fort Worth Star-Telegram*, December 16, 1962, p. 44; Austin American Statesman, December 16, 1962; Bob Rooker, "Slant-Hole Scandal Puts Oil in Legislature Spot," *The Dallas Morning News*, December 16, 1962, p. 8.

8. New Attorney General Waggoner Carr filed more similar suits in 1963, based on a penalty of $1,000 per day of production, totaling $689,445 asked. The state had collected $404,545 as of May 23, 1964. Most of the penalty judgments went unpaid and those unpaid judgments were dismissed for lack of prosecution.

9. Austin Bureau of The News, "Legislature Spurns Action On Slant-Holes, Small Tracts," *The Dallas Morning News*, June 2, 1963, p. 8.

10. "Jury Picked For Trial of 3 Oilmen," *The Dallas Morning News*, June 4, 1963, p. 4.

11. "Two Found Guilty in Slant Well Suit," *The Dallas Morning News*, June 28, 1963, p. 6.

12. "Fines Fixed by Court in Slant Case," *The Dallas Morning News*, September 4, 1963, p. 16.

CHAPTER 25
HUMBLE v. LONG

On Saturday, June 26, 1962, Humble filed its civil case against H. L. "Pete" Long and others in the Fourth District Court of Rusk County, where Judge Joe C. Gladney usually presided. Chapter 13 provides the background for this story.

This case was among six that Humble filed in Rusk County asking for damages totaling $1 million against alleged deviators. Two of these cases were against Long. Judge A. Royce Stout of Waxahachie replaced Judge Gladney on the bench for these cases because Gladney owned interests in Long's deviated wells. (1)

Long assembled the cream of East Texas's trial lawyers for his defense: Fred Erisman of Longview, Gordon Wellborn and Rex Houston of Henderson, and Angus Wynne of Dallas. Jack Flock of Tyler and Frank Heard of Dallas represented Humble, and Jack Moore represented Texaco, an intervenor in the case.

Pretrial hearings in the case began on Thursday, June 28. Long's counsel issued a subpoena for the chairman of the board of Humble, Morgan Davis, ordering him to appear with records of Humble's well locations in Rusk, Gregg, and Upshur counties. (2)

Billy Don O'Neal, the engineer in charge of reservoir operations for Humble, was first to testify. He said that most of the wells that he helped survey in the East Texas Field could not have been productive had they not been drilled on a slant.

Angus Wynne sought to elicit from O'Neal that oil flows through the Woodbine Sand from west to east in the East Texas Oil Field, and, therefore, any oil taken from Humble's lease via Long's deviated well(s) had been replaced by oil from the west. O'Neal acknowledged the easterly flow of oil in the Woodbine, but such flow was not uniform throughout the field. He implied that one could not depend on oil from the west to replace stolen oil. (3)

Hugh McKinley, Humble's field superintendent, told the court that mud suddenly began to appear in Humble's storage tanks on the Silvey lease. When workmen pulled the rods out of the Silvey A-22 well, they found the well full of fresh mud. He said the only well being drilled nearby was on Long's Mary Smith lease, clearly implying that Long's crooked well had intersected the Silvey A-22.

Don Barkman, a Railroad Commission employee in Kilgore, testified for the defense that he had run inclination tests on at least two of Long's wells and had found them to be within the three-degree limit. And, Shelby Guidrey, a Long employee, testified that he had tested some Long wells and found them capable of producing from 20 to 80 barrels of oil per day.

Albert Dawsey, a petroleum engineer from Tyler, testified for Long, stating that Humble had already produced more oil than had been originally in place beneath its Silvey lease, and that the easterly movement of oil within the Woodbine had kept the lease replenished with oil. (4)

On July 31, Judge Stout, in a related slant-hole case, granted Humble the right to test 16 wells on the J. R. Holt lease operated by Jack McCubbin and Rex Stegall. O'Neal reappeared to tell the court that he had found a number of wells to be deviated, including two of Long's, these being the subjects of Humble's suit against Long. He said that three wells on the Smith B lease tested as capable of producing a total of only three barrels of oil per day. Heard, representing Humble, asked O'Neal whether these wells were capable of producing at this rate, to which O'Neal replied, "Not with vertical well bores, no sir." O'Neal said that Long's Smith B-4 well was deviated by 60 degrees, the B-3 well at 66 degrees, and the B-11 well beyond the allowable three degrees. Wells 1 and 2 on the Smith A lease were also illegally deviated, but none of the wells on the C lease was illegal. (5)

After the close of the Humble v. Long hearing, the case lay dormant until it came to trial on February 11, 1963. Humble claimed actual damages against Long of $375,000 and asked for $100,000 in punitive damages. The case was unique in that Judge Stout, allowed Tom Perryman, then a partner with country singer Jim Reeves in radio station KGRI in Henderson, to record and broadcast live the closing arguments on February 20. (6)

Perryman, longtime host of the Tom Perryman Show at The Ranch (KKUS, 104.1 FM in Tyler), gave me a copy of his 1963 recording of the closing arguments and I sat down to listen to the trial in August 2009, 46 years after it first went out over the airwaves. (7) In addition to the presentation of their legal points, Long's lawyers—Fred Erisman, Gordon Wellborn, Rex Houston, and Angus Wynne—provided high theater in their pleadings. Wellborn sounded like an evangelical preacher, his voice rising to thunderous exhortation and falling to a solicitous near-whisper. Erisman and Wynne gave similar performances.

On Humble's team, Jack Flock and Frank Hurd presented their cases eloquently and calmly.

Judge Stout issued his charge to the jury in the form of 24 questions. Of these, the following four formed the bases of the rest:

5. Is Well Mary Smith #3 bottomed under Humble's lease?
6. Is Well Mary Smith #4 bottomed under Humble's lease?
7. Did Long cause Mary Smith well #2 to be drilled under Humble's lease?
8. Did Long so commingle oil that the amount of oil taken from Humble cannot be determined with reasonable certainty?

If the jury answered yes to any of these four questions, further answers would also be required. If all four questions were answered no, the remaining ones would be irrelevant, and Long would be relieved of liability.

The burden of proof in a civil case rests on the plaintiff, who must prove "by a preponderance of the evidence" its allegations. The defense need only convince the jury that the plaintiff's case is inadequate. In the present case, Humble alleged that Long had intentionally and maliciously: (a) drilled wells from lands under which there was no oil, (b) deviated said wells so as to extend into Humble's leases, (c) had stolen oil from Humble through said wells, and (d) thereby inflicted financial damage amounting to $375,000 upon Humble.

The defense attacked Humble and its case throughout the trial, as revealed in the summations:

Erisman noted that the (Eastman photographic) well-surveying equipment used to survey Long's wells, suspended on 2,000 feet of cable and requiring a 40-second exposure, could not be trusted because of vibration inherent in the suspending cable. Wellborn attacked Schlumberger's recalculation, after the fact, of survey results as attempts to make the results fit their claim. Wynne noted that Humble had drilled several deviated wells, citing Humble's specific permit for such wells, and had been put on notice by the Railroad Commission that Long had been granted a permit to drill replacement wells deviated from the vertical (but staying within his own lease). The defense claimed that Humble was duty-bound to prove exactly where the bottoms of Long's wells were, and that Humble was unable to do so when two surveys of the same well gave widely differing results.

Humble claimed that it had a number of experts who could testify regarding the accuracy of the well surveys, but they failed to bring those experts to court, casting doubt on their faith in their experts and/or the surveys. Flock claimed that Humble was surprised to learn of Long's drilling directional wells and that Humble had no notice of directional drilling in the East Texas Oil Field. Wynne rebutted, stating that Long had filed applications with the Railroad Commission to drill directional wells and that such applications are provided to operators of adjacent leases by the commission as a matter of course. Thus, Humble was legally put on notice.

The case went to the jury, with Herschel Christian of Henderson its foreman, on Thursday, February 21. The jury deliberated for seven hours before filing into the courtroom at 11:30 on Friday morning. When Judge Stout asked whether the jury had reached a verdict, Christian rose to his feet and said he and the 11 others had voted "no" to the four critical questions in the judge's instructions to them.

The courtroom erupted. Long and his lawyers celebrated. Judge Stout thundered as he gaveled the closure of the proceedings, "This is a rank miscarriage of justice!"

Judge Stout promised to reset the trial in Smith County where a local jury might be more inclined to impartiality. (8) The matter did come before the 114th District Court in Tyler where the parties filed an Agreed Judgment on July 25, 1967, in which Long agreed to pay Humble and Texaco $97,000, with Humble taking three quarters and Texaco, one quarter of the total. (9)

But there's more to the story.

In addition to the lawsuit filed by Humble against Long discussed here, Pan American and Socony Mobil filed suit against Long for theft via slanted wells on his Willie Starr lease at about the same time, in late June 1962. Long was already indebted to Southwestern Life Insurance Company. That's the same insurance company that lent Nortex Oil funds with which to buy crooked wells. Long, in need of cash, conveyed some of his oil properties to the insurance company under a deed of trust as additional security for his debt. Pete and his wife Virginia partitioned the community property and sold, subject to the deeds of trust, the same properties to Verde Oil Company for $30,000 cash on July 18, 1962. Pan Am and Mobil filed a second suit against Long for conveying assets to defraud his creditors.

The two major companies also sued Verde, seeking to recover either properties or money, claiming Long's conveyance to Verde was fraudulent and intended to deprive them of just recovery. They also claimed that Verde was on notice of Long's deceit and therefore that the sale to Verde should be voided. The district court in a nonjury trial found for the defendant Verde. Pan Am and Mobil appealed to the U.S. Fifth Circuit Court of Appeals, which under its chief judge, Griffin B. Bell, later U.S. attorney general in the Carter administration, upheld the district court's ruling for Verde in a ruling of October 25, 1966. (10)

The appellate court recognized Long's fraudulent act, but it agreed with the lower court's findings. According to the decision, Verde, although aware of Long's financial distress and his being involved in the slant-hole matter, had paid adequate compensation for the properties, and had exercised adequate, if little, diligence. Verde had no further obligation to investigate Long's fraud. Its cursory title examination stood as adequate, and plaintiffs failed to prove conclusively that Verde was obliged to have done more.

The Court of Appeals recognized the conflicting evidence as to Verde's obligation to investigate more deeply Long's fraudulent intent, but declined to overrule the district court judge.

NOTES

1. Fred, Pass, "Humble Moves Testing Rig Onto Tyler Oilman's Lease," *The Dallas Morning News*, July 11, 1962, p. 5.

2. East Texas Bureau of The News, "Officials Of Majors Summoned," *The Dallas Morning News*, June 20, 1962, p. 4.

3. Fred, Pass, "Hot Oil Testimony Under Way Despite Pleadings of Defense," *The Dallas Morning News*, June 29, 1962, p. 2.

4. Fred Pass, "Oilman Long Silent In Slant-Well Suit." *The Dallas Morning News*, June 30, 1962, p. 6.

5. Fred Pass, "Humble Wins Right To Run More Tests," *The Dallas Morning News*, August 1, 1962, p. 4.

6. It was New Year's Eve 1960; I was meeting my father for lunch in front of his office (in the Bramlette Building) in downtown Longview. He emerged from the building with two gentlemen– Tom Perryman and Jim Reeves. Perryman and Reeves had come to seek my dad's backing in their purchase of radio station KGRI in Henderson. The four of us had a genuinely pleasant conversation, and Reeves invited me to play guitar with his band that night's concert in Longview. Alas, I had another engagement and missed the opportunity of a lifetime. The date of Reeve's concert is verified in Larry Jordan, *Jim Reeves: His Untold Story*, p. 335; PageTurner Publishers, Chula Vista, CA, 2011.

7. Tom Perryman died on Thursday evening, January 11, 2018, at his home in Tyler. I will forever be grateful to Tom for his friendship that began when he called me to ask of a donation to one of his causes.

8. Fred Pass, "Judge Sets Aside Oil Case Verdict," *The Dallas Morning News*, February 23, 1963, p.5.

9. I thank Sandra Lyles of the Court's Records Office for bring me two boxes of the Court's records of the case on August 7, 2019.

10. Pan American Petroleum Corporation and Socony Mobil Oil Company, Inc., Appellants, v. Verde Oil Company, Inc., et. al., Appellees, 367 F.2d 461 (5th Cir.1966), October 25, 1966. https://law. justia.com/cases/federal/appellate-courts/F2/367/461/427890/ Accessed 6/4/2019, RC. A copy of the appeals court's decision is in my files.

CHAPTER 26
MOORE ON TRIAL

David Moore grew up in the oil field where his family had owned land and mineral interests. Royalties from oil production gave the family a comfortable life in Gladewater. When David finished law school, he pursued parallel careers, one in law and the other in a workover business operated by a partner. Every producing well has myriad problems, some major, others minor, but each requires serious attention. In many cases, a workover rig is employed. This is usually a small version of a drilling rig capable of pulling pipe out of the hole and returning it, but incapable of bearing the weight and torque necessary for drilling. Moore's association with the oilfield business was not made public. After law school, he was elected criminal district attorney of Gregg County and served from 1953 until 1955. That's when Governor Allan Shivers appointed him to complete Fred Erisman's unexpired term as judge of the 124th Judicial District of Texas, a post he held from 1955 through 1980. Moore continued in retirement to serve as visiting judge.

But he also invested in the drilling of oil wells, and in one important case, he allowed Jelly Scates to name him operator of the M. F. Fisher well.

The Moore family owned a lease in the Sabine River Bottom, just west of the Hays lease owned by my family. Although I don't recall any deep personal relationships between our families, we certainly knew each other. Given his family background in the oil patch and his ownership of a workover company, I am certain that Moore's knowledge of oilfield matters was significant. (1) Moore's son James told me that the Moores, Scateses, Murphys, and Maxwells had been longtime social friends. Social gatherings of these friends included reminiscences of the slant-hole days.

At the first hearing of the House General Investigating Committee, five suspected deviators took the stand and refused to testify on grounds of possible self-incrimination. But David Moore did testify. His testimony, as reported by the committee, was another exercise in "I just don't recall." Moore said that he, Tom Cook, and E. W. Scates acquired the one-acre M. F. Fisher lease just south of Lake Harris in Moore's name in consideration for their drilling a well on it. He turned the drilling of the well over to Scates and retained a one-eighth interest in the deal. He paid $7,000 as his share of the drilling and completion cost of the well, but although he was a second-generation oil operator, he couldn't explain why this well cost twice as much as did drilling and completing a straight well.

The committee counsel showed Moore a survey of his well that indicated it was kicked 2,510 feet at an angle of 49 degrees. Moore responded that his first knowledge of this was when he was served a restraining order preventing his going on the lease. When asked about his conversations with Scates after receiving the restraining order, Moore replied that Scates never told him anything about the well. Moore said that he had asked Scates whether the well was crooked and that Scates refused to answer. Moore told the committee that he did not press Scates further for an answer.

Moore said he'd bought the J. W. Free lease in 1958 after it had undergone a rapid decline in production. He and his partners evidently reworked the well as a slanted hole, and then produced oil for a while before Nelson Decker and L. D. Murphy curved it out. Moore and others then sold the curve-out for "more than $15,000." (2)

Robert V. Jobe owned a small interest in Moore's M. F. Fisher lease, but Moore didn't know who Jobe was, and he knew nothing about his interest in the lease. Jobe, as discovered later, was an alias used by L. Dwight Murphy, a Railroad Commission engineer.

Moore told the committee that he owned a one-eighth interest with Scates in the Sexton lease, on which the #4 well had been kicked 2,767 feet at 35 degrees. He failed to recall the price he paid Scates for his interest. Moore also testified that he learned of the kicked well "probably when I read about it in the paper." But he said he never discussed the matter with Scates.

Committee member Rep. Bill Hollowell of Grand Saline urged Moore to take a polygraph test, and Moore said he would consider doing so. However, Moore wrote Chairman Ballman on September 12 to say that he would decline the request.

Moore testified that by 1958 he had joined Tom Cook Jr. and Jelly Scates, both of whom knew the drilling business better than he, as a nonoperating partner, and he depended on Cook and Scates to handle the details of his investment in their projects. On occasion, Cook and Scates would buy leases or drill wells in Moore's name, not an uncommon practice.

Moore either knew or should have known of the illegal activity. Did he?

Scates refused on constitutional grounds to testify before the committee.

Of course, Moore's position as district judge made him a good target for exposure by a politically motivated attorney general. Had Moore been just another citizen, Wilson would probably have been far less inclined to make an example of him. Wilson sought out named operators, but not non-operating partners, in his pursuit of the guilty deviators, even though several of them were partners with full knowledge of all the slant-hole activity and not remotely innocent.

Moore demanded on the day he was indicted that he be tried immediately. His trial, the second criminal trial to come out of the slant-hole investigation, was set for Monday, February 25, 1963, with Judge Ward Chandler of Carthage on the bench in Moore's own courtroom. Judge Chandler denied the state's motion for a change of venue. The state claimed that it couldn't get a fair trial because of Moore's being well known and popular in Gregg County. The defense claimed that the indictment against Moore was improper because it should have been brought under a special provision in Texas law governing theft of minerals rather than under general theft law. The special mineral law provides that theft of minerals is a misdemeanor punishable by a fine up to $1,000.

Gregg County District Attorney Ralph Prince, a close personal friend of Moore's, refused to participate in the trial, leaving his assistants Nathan Holt and Kenneth Dickerson, along with Cecil Rotsch of the attorney general's office, to conduct the prosecution. Moore hired a team of East Texas lawyers, the first two of whom we have already met—Fred Erisman, Gordon Wellborn, R. L. Whitehead, and Bill Wilder. (3)

The defense presented a damning case against the prosecution. They stated that David McAngus, an assistant attorney general, and George Reed of the DPS had taken members of two Gregg County grand juries to lunch or dinner and had discussed the Moore case with them. Neither man denied the accusation. Dickerson denied knowledge of such meetings, but he admitted that he had met with three grand jurors at the home of one of them, but only after the indictments had been filed. Whitehead stated early in the trial that had Attorney General Wilson not personally "gone before the grand jury there never would have been this disgraceful indictment."

Erisman pointed out to the jury that the indictment of Moore involved only the M. F. Fisher well, and that each of three different counts in that indictment claimed that Moore's well was bottomed under each of three different adjacent leases. Therefore, the state didn't claim to know where Moore's well is, and without proof of its location, the state had no case.

James R. Staton of Eastman Oil Well Survey Company described the equipment used to determine the angle of inclination of a well and its direction. Erisman claimed that Eastman had run two well surveys but had presented only one at trial. Staton replied that only one survey had been run, but that after rechecking the results Eastman had corrected the errors, including the names of the men actually on the job. Wellborn objected to Staton's testimony as hearsay because Staton was not present at the well when the survey was run on June 10, 1962. Staton's son Jimmie, also an Eastman employee, testified that he and Rennie Picard had actually tested the Moore well. It was his first well survey. The elder Staton swore that the Eastman equipment would give results within an accuracy of 8 percent of the well's depth, but Erisman showed the jury that the steel of the casing would affect the compass readings. He waved a pin over the compass, inducing the needle to move several degrees.

Erisman forced the prosecution to admit that major oil companies had contributed "almost half a million dollars to finance the oil well testing and that the data had later been made available to the majors and was being used now against the independent operators." That testimony by Assistant Attorney General Bob Flowers surely helped sway the jury against the state and the majors.

The trial lasted four days, and on Thursday, February 28, Judge Chandler instructed the jury to return a verdict of "not guilty." The courtroom, crowded with about 175 of Moore's friends, erupted in applause. Moore had already expressed his confidence in being acquitted and thanked his supporters.

Judge Chandler castigated the grand jury for bringing the indictment, saying, "It is my opinion that the indictment in this case is a disgrace to the jury system on such evidence as presented here, and reflects careless and irresponsible conduct for apparent reasons other than those charged by the law." (4)

Judge Moore was on his bench the next morning and remained a popular district judge until his retirement at the end of 1980 after 25 years on the bench. He continued to preside over cases in Gregg and other counties until shortly before his death in November 1997.

NOTES

1. I thank James Moore, David Moore's son, for his generosity and for interviews in his home in Gladewater on February 24 and 26, 2016.

2. When a well begins to produce more than 100 barrels of salt water per day, the cost of disposing of that water could exceed the value of the limited amount of oil produced by the same well. By plotting the expected future production of oil from a well (or a lease), the Railroad Commission could estimate the total amount of oil that well or lease might eventually produce. Thus, potential production from a well or lease might be plotted or "curved-out" to give the operator a future allowable that could be transferred or sold. A curve-out of 6,000 barrels of oil could be sold at the market price for oil, then $2.50 per barrel, for $15,000. The curved-out well or lease would then be abandoned and the curve-out allowable produced from a different lease.

3. I did not know Mr. Whitehead. He and my father competed for leadership of the Gregg County Democratic Party, which was divided into conservatives (Cargill) and liberals (Whitehead.) Whitehead's son R. Laughton, Jr. is a noted divorce lawyer in Longview who represented me in a 1994 divorce.

4. See a series of articles in the *Longview Daily News*, February 25, 26, 27, and 28, and March 1, 1963.

We have already learned in Chapter 17 that L. Dwight Murphy transported bribes from the deviators to the Railroad Commission in Austin. Both the Gregg and Upshur County Grand Juries indicted Murphy on numerous counts. Murphy's trial on the charge of conspiracy to bribe began on July 9, 1963, in Judge Looney Lindsey's 115th District Court in Upshur County. (1)

Robert Smith, an assistant attorney general who led the prosecution, claimed in opening remarks that … "the state will produce evidence designed to show that Murphy and Longview oil operator E. W. Scates conspired to bribe [Robert] Matthews into conducting a false survey of the [Key Production RA] Akins [2A] well [in Upshur County], and that Matthews was paid $1,000." (2) In Chapter 17, we learned that Matthews had confessed his participation to commission chair Bill Murray in May 1962, at the same time implicating Murphy.

Murray fired Murphy, but allowed Matthews to resign from the commission. Smith based his case primarily on the testimony of Matthews after Judge Lindsey dismissed Matthews as a defendant on the motion of Upshur County DA Duncan so that he could testify against Murphy. Lindsey then denied the motion of Matthews' attorney J. W. Tyner who asked for a mistrial after Smith made reference to "the black hand of the defendant."

Testimony by a handwriting expert revealed that Murphy had signed bank deposits and checks as Robert V. Jobe, the alias used by Murphy in his nefarious work. C. E. Jennings of Pan American Petroleum testified that he saw 80 stands of pipe (about 4,800 feet) come out of the Adkins well, which had been permitted for 3,725 feet. Murphy and Matthews had reported to the commission that the well was straight. J. C. Staton of Eastman Well Survey Company stated that his survey of the well showed a deviation of 57 degrees and that the bottom of the well was

2,952 feet southwest from its surface location. It was a deviated well. On cross-examination, Staton admitted that the Eastman survey would have an error in direction of eight percent of the well's depth (3).

Arthur Barbeck, chief engineer of the Oil and Gas Division of the commission, told the court that he had hired Murphy in 1953 and had helped him receive a promotion in the Kilgore office. He also said "that Murphy had on many occasions in 1959 and 1960 reported the possibility of slanted wells in the East Texas Field and had made recommendations on how the commission could deal with the situation before the slant well inquiry broke."

Murphy testified in his own defense as the last witness. He "denied that he had considered, confederated, or combined with E. W. Scates... to bribe Robert Matthews." (4) The prosecutors argued that because a state employee was on trial, "This is only incidentally a slant-hole case," Smith said. "The main issue here is corruption in state government." Duncan told the jury, "...when trust and duty go astray, restitution is needed." (5)

The defense claimed that the state had not established evidence that a positive agreement had been made between Murphy and others; nor had the state proved that the alleged bribe had taken place in Upshur County.

The jury began deliberations at 2:50 p.m. on Friday, July 12, and returned its verdict at 7:15 p.m. Foreman D. G. Brasher announced the verdict—guilty of conspiracy in a bribe!—and set the sentence at two years. Judge Lindsey instructed the jurors to restudy the charge and make the wording of their verdict technically correct.

NOTES

1.   Judge Looney E. Lindsey was a native of Upshur County. He built a
     weekend house on top of an old oil derrick which was featured in numerous
     local and national news features. https://www.findagrave.com/
     memorial/27350784/looney-e_-lindsey. Accessed September 28, 2019.

2.   Fred Pass, "Testimony Begins in Oil Bribe Case," *The Dallas Morning News*,
     July 10, 1963, p. 9.

3.   *Baytown Sun*, July 12, 1963, www.newspapers.com/newspage/6484614.
     Accessed 12/10/2013, RC.

4.   Ibid.

5.   Fred Pass, "State Engineer Gets Two Years In Bribery Case," *The Dallas
     Morning News*, July 13, 1963.

6.   Austin Bureau of The News, "New Trial Ordered In Slant Well Case," *The
     Dallas Morning News*, April, 30, 1964, p. 10.

CHAPTER 28
MURRAY DUSTED

By 1962, Bill Murray had attempted to deal with the slant-hole drilling matter for about 10 years, and since 1961 as the sole active member of the Railroad Commission. (1), (2) His vacillation between aggressive investigator and wimp frustrated the Texas Rangers. On the other hand, the slant-hole drillers, angry with Murray for not stopping the investigation, threatened him with a campaign of dirt-digging in a clumsy attempt to have him protect them from themselves. (3)

Then it happened. The Austin Bureau of *The Dallas Morning News* got wind of an oil venture in Throckmorton County in which "Murray grossed more than $285,000, which he and three partners acquired July 1, 1958," as it reported on Monday, April 8, 1963. The same reporters wrote: "Public records on file in Throckmorton County indicate he invested little or nothing to obtain the lease." (4), (5) Waggoner Carr, who succeeded Wilson as attorney general, launched an investigation of Murray's oil interests that same day. *The Dallas Morning News* published another article the next day, stating that Murray et al. purchased the 8,500-acre lease "for what public records describe as $10, a drilling agreement and $425,000 to be paid out of production revenue." (6), (7) On Wednesday, Murray resigned his seat on the Railroad Commission, and on Friday, *The Dallas Morning News* ran an editorial that stated, "THE RECITATION of facts on the Murray case by this newspaper last Monday was not motivated by malice or ill will. ... The News never said he did anything wrong in its factual accounts of his Throckmorton oil dealings. ...We consider such reporting to be a part of our journalistic task..." (8) That same day saw *The Dallas Morning News* run another editorial, thanking NBC Radio reporter Morgan Beatty for his praise of them "last Monday night." Beatty said, "Yesterday *The News* printed the facts, let the chips fall where they would." (9)

The state's Code of Ethics, adopted in 1957, 10 years after Murray's appointment as commissioner, states that no officer or employee of a state agency "shall make personal investments in any enterprise which will create a substantial conflict between his private interests and the public interest." *The Houston Chronicle* commented, "The commission has no written policy on employee participation in the oil and gas business, but *The Chronicle* is told there has been a policy made known by word of mouth for years. That policy is that commission employees cannot have outside oil and gas interests; they cannot work for oil and gas companies during hours or after hours; they cannot be in the leasing business, but if an employee happened to inherit family oil and gas property, that would be alright." (10)

Johnny Mitchell, President of the Texas Independent Royalty Owners and Producers Association (TIPRO) in 1963, wrote a scathing letter to *The Dallas Morning News*, published on April 14, 1963, in which he accused the News of character assassination, claiming the attack on Murray was "an astonishing misuse of its enormous news reporting powers." (11)

Murray's oil and gas dealings while a commissioner certainly did result in profit for him and his partners. The question is whether a regulator should have business dealings in the regulated industry. Most regulators are lawyers and/or political wannabes with little or no background in the subject being regulated. Murray was the first member of the Railroad Commission whose training and experience had been in oil and gas, the only business he had ever known. Other commissioners with professions outside the oil business continued their business affairs, but Murray had nowhere to go to supplement his state salary except the business he knew and loved. And to my own personal knowledge, oil men of both Big Oil and Little Oil were glad to have a man of Murray's knowledge of the industry serving on the commission.

Murray and his partners earned significant profits by buying leasehold interests rejected by others and developing production from those interests at substantial financial risk. Two of Murray's oil deals—one in Throckmorton County and one in Wharton and Brazoria counties, both outlined below—made newspaper headlines that ultimately brought him down.

In the Throckmorton deal, Murray and partners acquired some 8,500 acres of leasehold on July 1, 1958, with Murray's portion being one-sixth. They agreed to pay as follows: (a) $425,000 in oil payments out of 85 percent of production, if any, (b) to drill at least five new wells within 12 months, and (c) an option allowing assignors to repurchase a one-quarter interest in the property for $5,000 after the oil payment had been liquidated. (12) Murray et al. paid the required $425,000 and drilled as many as 25 new wells at their own risk and expense before they sold half the property within two years for $742,000. Murray sold the remaining half of his one-sixth interest on August 1, 1960, before the slant-hole affair raised its ugly head publicly in 1962, for $135,000. (His minimum expense, not counting costs of drilling the wells, was his one-sixth of $425,000, or about $71,000. His profit was his one-sixth of the $742,000, about $125,000, plus the $135,000, less his cost of $71,000, for a total of $190,000, adjusted by any profit or loss from the 25 new wells.) (13)

Jimmy Banks, who ran the Austin Bureau of *The Dallas Morning News*, also reported that Murray and others had bought leases in Wharton and Brazoria counties, where others had drilled dry holes. There they drilled about 10 successful wells and sold them, with Murray's earning a profit in excess of $200,000. (14)

A week after his resignation from the commission, Murray declared, "I had said for many years I intended to resign from the commission. Each time, I was persuaded to stay a little longer." (15)

Carr's grand jury refused to indict Murray on June 18. In its report, the grand jury stated, "We abhor the publicity and news releases in regards to the William J. Murray matter." Carr responded, saying, he was "greatly surprised that the grand jurors criticized the right of the public to know." (16) Carr must have forgotten that grand jury proceedings are legally secret.

Murray had, in fact, submitted to a polygraph examination administered by the DPS on May 16, 1962. Furthermore, Col. Garrison had already announced that Murray's answers to questions were truthful. In particular, Murray had never: (1) had an interest in an East Texas deal; (2) been offered an interest in an East Texas deal; (3) received a proposal in the way of a bribe or payoff to call off the inclination and directional surveys…; (4) received money from an operator; and (5) received any campaign contributions since 1948. (17) And he had told *The Longview Daily News* that he had passed the polygraph test in May. (18)

When Robert Nieman interviewed Ranger Jim Ray in 1997, Ray told him about how Murray failed the polygraph test.

The following is the relevant portion of the interview transcript:

JIM RAY: …And we did get the chairman of the Railroad Commission to resign.
ROBERT NIEMAN: Well did it go that high?
JIM RAY: Yeah. Run him on polygraph.
ROBERT NIEMAN: He didn't pass?
JIM RAY: No. Old boy named Bill Murray.
ROBERT NIEMAN: Bill Murray?
JIM RAY: Yeah.
ROBERT NIEMAN: He was a railroad commissioner?
JIM RAY: Chairman of the Railroad Commission.

By the time of Nieman's interview in 1997, Ray was 83 and perhaps his memory was faulty. Murray *did* resign in April 1963, but certainly not because of a failed polygraph test. (19)

The 1967 Arab-Israeli War revealed how far the Texas oil industry had declined. As in previous times of crisis, Texas ramped up to full production in order to fill the shortage in global crude. For the first time, Texas proved unequal to the challenge. Many mature wells proved incapable of meeting their allowables. Murray, then president of TIPRO, warned "there is essentially no net spare efficient producing capacity in this entire nation." (20) That is, the United States had inadequate capacity to produce the oil it consumed.

A test conducted in 1971 to demonstrate Texas's capacity to produce two million extra barrels a day failed, revealing that the reserve capacity was only one-tenth that amount. The test proved Murray right.

Murray continued to serve the oil and gas industry that he loved until his death in August 2004. In 1973, he chaired what later became the Energy

Reliability Council of Texas (ERCOT). In 1989, his industry admirers established the William J. "Bill" Murray Endowed Chair of Engineering at the University of Texas. In recognition of his service to the state of Texas, Murray was buried in the Texas State Cemetery in Austin. (21)

In my opinion, the state of Texas lost the services of a dedicated, if politically naïve, servant who did more good for the state than most statewide office holders. Whether his downfall resulted from a smear campaign launched by the slant-hole drillers, as Murray died claiming, will not likely ever be proved. The uproar around his oil dealings, well-known within the oil industry that he regulated, certainly helped sell newspapers. I just don't know whether Murray took bribes, although he knew that illegal wells were being drilled. He didn't have the necessary political skill to deal with an enterprise as challenging as the slant-hole matter.

NOTES

1. Jim Drummond, *Oil Daily*, April 11, 1961.

2. Jim Drummond, *Oil Daily*, June 22, 1961

3. Dawson Duncan, "Murray Says Investigator Hired to Seek 'Dirt' on Him," *The Dallas Morning News*, July 3, 1962, p. 1.

4. Fred Pass and Jimmy Banks, "Rail Commissioner Murray Grossed $285,000 on West Texas Oil Lease," *The Dallas Morning News*, April 8, 1963, p. 1.

5. Austin Bureau of The News, "Chronology Lists Deals On Murray's Oil Lease," *The Dallas Morning News*, April 8, 1963, p. 8.

6. Jimmy Banks, "Carr's Staff Launches Probe O Murray Oil Lease Interest." *The Dallas Morning News*, April 9, 1963, p. 1.

7. The Banks and Duncan reports cited the usual (in Texas, at least) purchase price of $10 without noting that under Texas law, one need not divulge the real price at which a property is conveyed. Stating a nominal sum, here $10, indicates that a valuable consideration, whether stated or not, has been paid for the property being traded.

8. Unsigned Editorial, "The Murray Case," *The Dallas Morning News*, April 12, 1963, p. 2.

9. Unsigned Editorial, "Thank You, Mr. Beatty," *The Dallas Morning News*, April 12, 1963, p. 2 Beatty told his audience that Murray et al., paid only $10 for the 8,500-acre lease.

10. Unsigned Editorial, *The Houston Chronicle*, April 15, 1963.

11. "TIPRO Head Accuses News Of Character Assassination," *The Dallas Morning News*, April 14, 1963, p. 4.

12. Murray's total cost in the property was a sixth of the original $425,000 plus his costs in the wells drilled. Drilling successful wells often leads to high profits, but drilling unsuccessful wells can be catastrophic.

13. The documents by which these transfers of property took place may be found in the Throckmorton County Clerk's Office in Throckmorton, Texas. I am grateful to Kay Cook of that office for helping me find and copy the relevant assignments during the week of July 28, 2014.

14. Jimmy Banks, "Murray Lists More Profits From Oil Deals," *The Dallas Morning News*, April 18, 1963, p. 1.

15. Austin Bureau of the News, "Murray, Tracing Ventures Can't Recall All His Deals," *The Dallas Morning News*, April 18, 1963, p. 7.

16. Grand Jury Clears Murray In Oil Case," *Brownwood Bulletin* (Brownwood, Texas) June 19, 1963, p. 12, accessed August 14, 2014, at http://www.newspapers.com, image #6692564.

17. "DPS Experts Are Called in Jury Probe," *The Times* (Shreveport, LA), April 17, 1963, p. 20.

18. "Murray Says Private Probe Seeking 'Dirt'," *Longview Daily News*, July 3, 1963.

19. Robert Nieman, *Texas Ranger Hall of Fame E-Book* (2006), Waco, Texas: Texas Ranger Hall of Fame and Museum.

20. "Tipro Chooses Murray," *The Dallas Morning News*, June 10, 1969, p. 12.

21. See www.cemetery.state.tx.us/pub/user_form822.asp?apers_id=8520 for Murray's obituary.

CHAPTER 29
CONTINENTAL v. AMTEX

Samedan Oil had farmed out parts of its Bob Wood lease to Amtex Oil in 1960, retaining an override of 13.75 percent. Amtex drilled 11 deviated wells on the farmed-out lands into Continental Oil's T. B. Harris to the west. (1)

Continental filed suit against Carter-Jones Drilling and Amtex Oil on June 20, 1962, in Gregg County, claiming "diversion of oil by deviated well bores" from their Harris lease and seeking damages of $320,000. Judge Sam Hall granted Continental a temporary restraining order to prevent the defendants from plugging their crooked wells.

Two days later, the defendants filed a countersuit in which they claimed damages of $10-million and that the restraining order would "constitute unreasonable search and seizure" of their property and a "reckless invasion of the rights of privacy of the defendants." (2)

On July 12, Continental filed a motion for summary judgment. Continental attached to its motion a formal report of a survey on one of the Amtex Bob Wood wells along with data and drawings that purported to prove that the well was deviated.

I have examined these logs and directional surveys. The suspect wells clearly extended into Continental's Harris lease. (3) The parties agreed on July 18, 1962, that five Continental wells and 11 Amtex wells would be surveyed for deviation. (4) But nothing appeared in the local newspapers about Continental Oil v. Amtex for more than a year.

In February 1963, a Rusk County jury denied Humble Oil any recovery from H. L. Long, even though there had been no question that Long's wells were clearly bottomed in Humble's lease. That convinced Waggoner Carr that he would never win a case in civil or criminal trials in East Texas courts. The major companies arrived at the same conclusion.

I discussed the slant-hole affair with Archie Tehan, Atlantic Oil's field superintendent at the time of the slant-hole events. He had known my father well. Tehan had earned his degree in petroleum engineering at the University of Wyoming in 1953 after having served as a combat crewman on a PBY Catalina "flying ship" in World War II. His duty ended on Okinawa. (5)

Tehan told me his management decided that in order to win a case against the deviators, they would be forced to prove exactly where an offending well was bottomed. That was impossible to accomplish in 1962. Evidently, Continental came to a similar conclusion. The company realized, as did Atlantic, that winning a case against a deviator in Gregg County was unlikely. The two sides filed motions to dismiss their suits, and Judge Sam Hall signed the motions on November 13, 1963, Bob Wood's 75th birthday.

Tehan said Atlantic recognized risks associated with challenging suspected slanted wells, because doing so would require proof of their own bottom hole locations. Because drilling a straight hole was impossible, he knew that some of Atlantic's wells might be bottomed outside the lease and thus illegal.

Atlantic only challenged Bull Barber and Doug Godfrey, deviators who operated leases near Atlantic's Sabine River Bottom leases. Some of Atlantic's wells there experienced unusually large declines in production, leading the company to suspect the sharp decline resulted from the siphoning of Atlantic's oil by slanted wells drilled by Godfrey and Barber.

Tehan also told me that the Marginal Well Rule, the loophole that made slant-hole drilling so attractive, pushed both Atlantic and Humble to install "back-pressure valves." These illegal valves would choke back a well to less than 20 barrels per day, making it a marginal well that could produce 18 barrels per day every day. Thus, Big Oil was skirting the law just as the deviators were. They were experts at whipstocking wells, he told me, but he did not say that any of the majors actually drilled crooked wells.

NOTES

1. See Chapter 12.

2. Fred Pass, "4 East Texas Operators Sue Majors for 10 Million Dollars," *The Dallas Morning News*, June 23, 1962, p. 5.

3. I spent several hours reviewing the files of the Continental-Amtex litigation in the office of the Gregg County District Clerk. I no longer remember the date.

4. "CONOCO WELLS WILL BE SURVEYED AT KILGORE," *Fort Worth Star-Telegram*, July 19, 1962, p. 17.

5. Personal interview with Archie Tehan at The Butcher Shop in Longview on July 8, 2010.

CHAPTER 30
CARGILL'S STONE LEASE

The E. E. Stone lease, operated by my father between 1960 and 1962, produced oil from the adjoining T. G. Pressley lease. Sun Oil owned the Pressley lease, and filed suit against Cargill and his partners in federal court in Tyler in December 1963. (1) Sun alleged that the two Stone wells produced a total of 46,707 barrels of stolen oil between their completion and their being severed from the pipeline on July 30, 1962, and claimed the alleged theft resulted in damages of "$135,000 ($2.89 per barrel), or more." (2)

Cargill denied any control of the operations of either well before he assumed operations on August 1, 1960, and he denied that he knew or should have known the wells were deviated into Sun's lease. Even I don't believe that.

He asserted that the events claimed by Sun had occurred more than two years before Sun instituted the suit and therefore, the action was barred by the statute of limitations (Article 5526 of the Revised Civil Statutes of Texas.)

He also claimed that Sun's superior knowledge of and acquaintance with oil field activities should have made Sun aware of any deviated wells that might have been drilled into Sun's lease. Therefore, he claimed Sun was guilty of legal delays in its having not asserted its claims prior to Cargill's assumption of operations. By this argument, Sun had acquiesced in any taking claimed by Sun and had waived any rights to sue.

Finally, he noted that the water drive of the East Texas Oil Field pushed oil from the west eastward to replace oil removed from the east side of the field. Thus, Sun had not actually lost any oil. Its lease had the same amount of oil under it after the alleged theft that it had had previously. Therefore, Sun, having lost no oil or value, should recover nothing. (3)

Cargill eventually settled the suit with Sun by paying damages of $10,250. At the time of settlement, Cargill handed the attorneys for the oil companies a letter from Fugitt Realty Company. (4). It told of a client willing to pay Cargill $750 per acre for a 540-acre tract he owned and that was not involved in the slant-hole matter but lay in the middle of the East Texas Field. Sun, Atlantic, and Pan American, as well as other major companies, had miles of pipelines covering the surface of this tract. The potential buyer insisted that all pipelines be buried. Cargill notified the oil companies that state law required such pipelines be buried below plow depth—typically three feet—and, in light of such law, as well as the potential buyer's requirement, he must insist that the lines be buried. This new circumstance brought all the parties to agree to surface leases that, for an annual payment, allowed the major companies to maintain their pipelines on the surface, and relieved Cargill of any other obligation to the oil companies. I sold that tract to a cousin in the early 1990s.

Archie Tehan, introduced in the previous chapter, told me in our interview that his boss, Hooks Whittington, learned early on that the best way to deal with Cargill was through cooperation, unless his demands were too excessive. Cargill was known to be an expert in finding loopholes in leases and contracts, and he was willing to make life miserable for uncooperative parties if provoked. Tehan told me my father actually did Atlantic a favor by forcing the issue of above-ground flow lines and forcing Atlantic to replace its lines. Shortly thereafter, new environmental rules would have forced the replacement of leaking flow lines at a much greater expense to Atlantic.

Fred Pass of the Dallas Morning News published a piece about my father in July 1963, the opening sentence of which reads, "Nearly every property owner in Longview has oil income today because of the oil-finding wizardry of Robert Cargill." (5)

NOTES

1. See Chapter 12, Notes 1-4.

2. The details of Case #4171, Sun Oil v. Robert Cargill, are contained in the files of the Federal Court in Tyler, and I have a copy of these files. I base this report on the facts contained in these files.

3. Clark and Halbouty, in *The Last Boom* (pg. 278,) dispute this claim.

4. I have a copy of the Fugitt letter in my files.

5. Fred Pass, "East Texas Notebook," *The Dallas Morning News*, July 9, 1963, p.12. All of the wells mentioned in the article were legitimate wells.

CHAPTER 31 THE SIX-MILLION-DOLLAR
SWINDLE, II

In the spring of 1964, it appeared Nortex had won at least a significant portion of its $6 million back; but the story doesn't end there.

Nortex sued former shareholders of Ebro in April 1964, based on the 1962 judgment in which the District Court in Dallas had awarded Nortex nearly $4 million. (1) The losers filed an appeal in September 1964 that led to Nortex's losing its judgment. (2)

In a separate case, Nortex sued Schlumberger in Judge Owen Giles' court in Dallas claiming that Schlumberger was a participant in a civil conspiracy that resulted in injury to Nortex, but Giles allowed Schlumberger's request to have the trial moved to Houston, its home territory. (3), (4) Evidence presented at trial proved that Schlumberger had knowingly logged and perforated illegally slanted wells on Trust Oil leases now owned by Nortex, and that Schlumberger's engineers had filed false reports for Trust Oil claiming the wells were legal. Schlumberger stopped including depths of wells on its service orders in 1960— knowing that any well with more than 3,700 feet of pipe was certainly deviated. The new policy had the operator write the well's depth on a separate piece of paper which, after Schlumberger's charges had been calculated, was destroyed. Schlumberger adjusted logs of crooked wells to make them appear legitimate. The company also destroyed many of the logs in its files that were two years and older in 1964—in other words, logs of deviated wells. This appears to constitute deliberate destruction of evidence of Schlumberger's knowing participation in the drilling and logging of illegal wells.

Schlumberger's division manager said that as a firm, the service company was not the policeman of the oil patch and it was not Schlumberger's job to see that operators had proper permits for drilling directional wells.

The court record showed that Schlumberger's field engineer, B. J. Hallmark, who certified at least one of my father's slanted wells as straight, logged an average of one deviated well per week for a period of 18 months in the East Texas Oil Field.

Although Schlumberger's knowing participation in the slant-hole drilling was established in court, the trial court judge excluded the evidence of Schlumberger's acts as irrelevant to the case as filed—a conspiracy case. The court then determined the remaining evidence failed to demonstrate Schlumberger's participation in a conspiracy. Schlumberger had argued that it was the drilling of the illegally slanted wells that constituted a conspiracy if there was one, not its acts of two years prior to the sale to Nortex. Nortex appealed to the Civil Court of Appeals in Waco, where the trial court's decision was reversed and remanded for retrial. Schlumberger appealed to the Texas Supreme Court, which reversed the Court of Civil Appeals and rendered judgment for Schlumberger stating that Schlumberger was not a party to the fraudulent sale to Nortex some two years after its (Schlumberger's) acts. Only the sellers could be co-conspirators. (5)

Nortex just couldn't catch a break.

There's a saying in Texas: "You can get justice in lots of places, but the courthouse ain't one of 'em." (6)

NOTES

1. Don Millsap, "Settlement Reached In Slant-Well Suit," *The Dallas Morning News*, March 4, 1964, p. 12.

2. "Testimony Begins in Slant Suit," *The Dallas Morning News*, October 5, 1965, p 3.

3. "Trial Going To Houston," *The Dallas Morning News*, October 9, 1965, p. 11.

4. "Testimony Starts On Nortex Oil' Damages Suit," *The Dallas Morning News*, September 14, 1966, no page given.

5. Schlumberger Well Surveying Corporation v. Nortex Oil and Gas Corporation, 435 S.W.2d 854 (1968), No. B-443, Supreme Court of Texas.

6. See the PBS program *Justice For Sale*, which can be found at http://www.pbs.org/wgbh/pages/frontline/shows/justice/etc/synopsis.

The Stroud brothers had been under federal indictment (109 counts) as noted in Chapters 17 and 22. They came to trial in spring 1964 before Judge Joe Sheehy who dismissed 92 of the 109 counts and fined each brother $7,500 for violating the Connally Hot Oil Act. (1) Then Billy Bridewell and R. H. Hedge pleaded guilty to misdemeanor counts and paid fines of $5,000 each. (2) Bridewell had already settled with Continental Oil for $200,000. See Chapter 17 for more details. (3)

The Texas Court of Criminal Appeals heard L. D. Murphy's appeal of his conviction on March 10, 1964. The court unanimously reversed the conviction on April 29. Judge W. A. Morrison, writing for the court, stated:

> It must be remembered that this is a conspiracy case and not one for the offense of bribery. The fact that (Robert) Matthews and (E. W.) Scates were seen together at the well is not sufficient corroboration. Nor would the fact that both Murphy and Scates had an interest in a bank account and that Scates may have paid part of the costs of drilling a well be sufficient corroboration of Matthews' testimony that Murphy and Scates conspired together to bribe him. The state has failed to meet the requirements of (the law) in that the testimony of the accomplice witness has not been corroborated to show that Scates entered into an agreement with Murphy to bribe Matthews.

Matthews' testimony, as "an admitted wrongdoer" needed far more corroboration than the prosecution had provided.

And so, the appellate court ordered a new trial for Murphy. (4)

One lesson from the Murphy trial is that the evidence required to sustain a conviction for conspiracy is greater than that for a conviction of bribery. Seasoned prosecutors should have known that before they guided a grand jury in its indictment.

Murphy never went to trial again. The matter, like an old soldier, just faded away.

On October 30, 1963, an Austin jury assessed $12,800 against Harry Harrington, Charles Lutes, and Reid Allgood for drilling a deviated well in Wood County. It also levied $292,000 against these three, plus John Baton, for producing oil illegally for 10 years from the well. In this, the first of many penalty suits that came to trial, the penalty was calculated based on $80 per day of production for 3,650 days. (5) The defendants appealed the judgments to the Third Court of Civil Appeals (of Texas). Judge Robert W. Hughes handed down a 36-page ruling for the court on November 18, 1964, that upheld the lesser of the judgments, but ordered a new trial in the larger one because the state did not prove the number of days of the well's production, the basis of the assessed penalty.

The court also said, "...it was not incumbent upon the state to allege or prove that the well was knowingly deviated or drilled to a bottom-hole location off the lease...the legislature deliberately negatived [sic] the requirement that knowledge on the part of the violator is essential to infliction of penalties provided by it." Hughes also ruled that the because state need not prove intent, the commission cannot require intent in such cases.

Hughes' ruling established that civil penalty suits are provided for in Railroad Commission procedures, and are therefore legal and useful tools for enforcing commission rules. (6)

Harrington, et al., appealed the Court of Appeals decision to the Texas Supreme Court, but found no relief there. On October 12, 1966, the High Court said the uncontroverted evidence showed the well was operated for more than 10 years; therefore, the assessed penalty of $80 per day of operation ($292,000) was certainly legal because the trial jury had assessed the $80-per-day penalty instead of the maximum of $1,000 per day for such violations. (7)

John Wrather's slant-hole activity went beyond East Texas to Jackson County on the Gulf Coast south of Houston and Karnes County southeast of San Antonio. Carr and Wrather came to an agreed settlement on August 14, 1964, covering seven deviated wells in these South Texas counties and in Rusk and Gregg counties. Wrather paid the agreed-upon $118,825, bringing the total collected for penalty judgments to $953,595. That's a small portion of the $25.5 million assessed against the deviators. (8)

Pete Long's battles with Big Oil didn't end with his victory in the trial discussed in Chapter 25. Visiting Judge A. R. Stout angrily stated that the jury's verdict in favor of Long in the case of Humble Oil, et al., v. H. L. Long, et al., was "a rank miscarriage of justice!" He announced he would have the case retried in Smith County's 114th District Court. I went to the District Clerk's Records facility in Tyler on August 7, 2019, where two large boxes awaited me. They were filled with documents produced in the case. I ultimately found an agreed judgment dated July 25, 1967, in which the parties agreed that Long, et al., would pay to Humble, et al., $97,000, with ¾ going to Humble as plaintiff, and ¼ going to Texaco as intervenor. (9) That Judge Galloway Calhoun dismissed the case on February 2, 1971, leads me to think Long never paid the judgment.

The reluctance of local district attorneys to pursue the indictments handed down by their grand juries frustrated AG Carr sufficiently that he asked those DAs to dismiss all outstanding criminal indictments. I have visited the district clerks' offices in Gregg and Rusk counties to review the dismissals recorded there. The dismissals of all indictments issued by the Gregg County Grand Jury on December 11, 1962, covering dates from August 6, 1964 through March 6, 1966 (112 separate documents, some covering more than one individual), reside in the Gregg County District Clerk's office. Each dismissal is stamped, "Dismissed on State's Motion." (10)

Similarly, Carr asked the District Court of Rusk County to dismiss indictments of 11 of the deviators on February 5, 1965, and of another three on May 26, 1966, "because the evidence is insufficient to obtain or support a conviction." Judge J. C. Gladney was only too happy to agree. I am certain that the indictments against the remaining six individuals were likewise dismissed, but I did not locate the appropriate documentation for these cases. (11), (12)

With the election in November 1966 of Crawford Martin to succeed Carr as attorney general, the word spread that the new AG would pursue the deviators with more vigor than Carr had and would refuse to settle remaining slant-hole cases on lenient terms. Thirty of the deviators then initiated discussions of settlements of their penalty suit judgments. Carr signed agreed judgments in 21 cases for a total of $391,925 instead of the millions that might have been pursued (at $1,000 per day of operation per well) on December 31, 1966, the day his term expired. These settlements left 26 other cases still pending. (13)

The "Slant-Hole Scandal" died quietly, much like the proverbial month of March, "In like a lion; out like a lamb." It faded away with little or nothing done to punish the deviators. Why? Fred Pass provided some answers as early as 1964. (14) These include: (a) the Legislature's rule that the presiding judge in a case in which a lawyer-legislator is involved must delay the case until the legislative session is over; (b) the technical impossibility, at the time, of determining the exact location of the bottom of the hole made it easy for attorneys to destroy arguments by plaintiffs' lawyers about just where the wellbore is; (c) the public relations of the major oil companies had created more enemies than friends in "at least two of the counties involved"; (d) the aggressive Will Wilson lost his job as attorney general and was replaced by a less-enthusiastic Waggoner Carr; (e) Upshur County District Attorney Ott Duncan, the least-reluctant of the four district attorneys to pursue slant-hole indictments, lost his bid for re-election in 1964; (f) some of the major companies lost their appetites for lawsuits; (g) local businesses were dependent upon the health of the oil business, and were being hurt by the scandal's negative publicity; and (h) the state of Texas had inadequate laws against oil theft.

I had lunch on November 23, 2010, with former Gregg County District Attorney Rob Foster. Foster is a native of Longview and has been connected with Gregg County politics all his life. Rob told me that David Moore had a party just after Waggoner Carr dismissed the slant-hole indictments in 1964 for a large number of deviators. Invitations to Moore's party stated, "If you ain't indicted, you ain't invited!"

TIPRO, the advocacy group for independent oil interests, re-elected Robert Cargill, who had drilled six deviated wells, as its secretary at its summer meeting in 1968; and, in 1969, elected Bill Murray, the deposed Chairman of the Railroad Commission, as its president. The scandal was indeed dead. (15), (16)

NOTES

1. "Oil Men Fined $7,500 Each In Tyler Court," *Fort Worth Star-Telegram*, April 18, 1964, p.5.

2. Fred Pass, "The Slanted Well Scandals: What's Become of Them?", *The Dallas Morning News*, May 23, 1964, p. 8.

3. Fred Pass, "Slanted Oilwell Scandals Expected to Come to Boil," *The Dallas Morning News*, April 15, 1963, p. 17. These two articles by Fred Pass give a good, brief review of the Slant-Hole story through May 1964.

4. Austin Bureau of the News, "New Trial Ordered In Slant Well Case," *The Dallas Morning News*, April 30, 1964, p 10. One must wonder why the prosecution failed to seek a conviction on a charge of bribery instead of conspiracy to commit bribery.

5. "$304,800 Assessed Slant Defendants," *The Dallas Morning News*, October 31, 1963, p. 1.

6. "State Officials Elated Over Slant Well Appeals Ruling," *Fort Worth Star-Telegram*, November 19, 1964, p. 26.

7. The Austin Bureau of The News, "Court Upholds Penalties Fixed in Slant-Hole Cases," *The Dallas Morning News*, October 13, 1966, p. 12.

8. Austin Bureau of The News, "$118,823, Judgment Paid in Slant Case," *The Dallas Morning News*, August 15, 1964, p. 8.

9. I am grateful to Sandra Lyles of the Smith County District Clerk's office for locating the files of this and other cases for me on August 7, 2019.

10. Thanks to my assistant Marianne Edwards for finding and copying the dismissals in Gregg County on July 31, 2019.

11. I thank Samantha Ware of the Rusk County District Clerk's Office for finding the records for these dismissals for me on August 7, 2019.

12. I did not go to Wood or Upshur counties, but I am certain that indictments of indictments in those counties were also dismissed.

13. Jimmy Banks, "Departing Carr Settles 21 Suits," *The Dallas Morning News*, December 31, 1966, p.4.

14. Fred Pass, "The Slanted Well Scandals: What's Become of Them?" *The Dallas Morning News*, May 23, 1964, p. 8.

15. Jay Hall, "Joint Action Urged At TIPRO Parley," *The Dallas Morning News*, May 28, 1968, p. 9.

16. "TIPRO Chooses Murray," *The Dallas Morning News*, June 10, 1969, p. 12.

CHAPTER 33
TURK

John George, generally known in Longview as Turk, was among those indicted in the slant-hole investigations. A giant of a man, Turk's Lebanese heritage gave him a swarthy complexion and his hands were the size of hams. His father had come from Darbishtar, Lebanon, via Vera Cruz, in 1907 to the U.S. where the family name of Shaluly underwent Anglicization. The elder gentleman became Joseph J. George. After a year in his new country, the newly-named Mr. George wanted to settle down with a family. The Lebanese bachelor returned to to his homeland to find a wife. He returned with Grace, a Lebanese woman who had been educated in Canada. The couple settled in Waco where they opened George's Grocery.

Joseph and Grace produced six children, of whom John was the fourth, born in 1912. John quit school in the seventh grade to support the family by doing whatever jobs were available: delivering the newspaper, working in the family store, baking bread at the local bakery, or swamping—loading and unloading—on the beer truck.

Turk was a superb athlete: an avid bowler, golfer, and baseball player. He played semi-pro baseball in the Oklahoma League where, with his huge hands, he was a dominating pitcher. With his outgoing personality, he had a way with people and was a superb salesman. He had a great flair for entertaining and telling jokes and was always the life of any party. He was a big flirt and always had a bevy of girls following him, as seen by the scrapbook he kept from his army days: the stereotypical "girl in every port."

Turk survived the D-Day landing at Normandy and was decorated for bravery in action. He took a German bullet in a knee, which earned him a Purple Heart. Late in Turk's life, he told me his war stories, relishing those old memories and recounting them at any opportunity. He had hoped to return to professional baseball after the war; but the

German bullet to the knee ended those hopes. The New York Yankees and the Cincinnati Reds signed him as a scout for a number of years after the war, however.

Turk returned from the battlefields of Europe to Waco where he married Anne Marie Ritchie in January 1946. They settled in Tyler, but after a year, Turk moved Anne and baby daughter Patricia to Longview where he opened his bar, the Brass Rail, across Methvin Street from the post office and Conrad Hilton's second hotel, the Longview Hilton. This location gave the Brass Rail access to the local movers and shakers who would assemble at the hotel for breakfast or collect mail from the nearby post office.

During his career, Turk was at his best when coaching boys in any sport. It was this aspect of his life that eventually resurfaced in the Slant-Hole affair. He coached bowling, baseball, and, even some football. The young athletes and their parents loved Turk because he taught the boys good technique, team play, and respect.

At the Brass Rail, Turk hosted a cross section of Longview society; but his favorites were the oilmen: Clark Sample Sr. and Clark Jr., George Joseph, Bluford Stinchcomb, Tom Cook Sr. and Tom Jr., Tom Harris, Tracy Flanagan, Pete Cashell, my dad, Robert Cargill, as well as a number of others. The oil crowd was often at the Rail swapping tall tales about their latest big hits and dry holes. Ranger Glenn Elliott, Sam Andrews, and Longview newspaper publisher Carl Estes were also among Turk's close friends.

Bluford Stinchcomb was a handsome dandy who always wore fashionable suits. He was also a difficult and abrasive fellow. But Julian Hurst, owner of the Ford dealership in Longview was a close friend of his. Bluford could often be found at the dealership visiting with Julian. One day, Bluford was in Hurst's office when Ford representatives showed up to evaluate the dealership. There sat Bluford with his feet propped up on Julian's desk while the Ford reps asked questions. At some point, one of the Ford men had had enough of this lazy "salesman" and confronted Bluford with, "Well, just how many Fords have you sold or tried to sell today?" Bluford rose up slowly, adjusted his belt, and said, "Not a goddamn one because they are too goddamn high and they aren't worth a damn, anyway!"

Bluford liked to go into places where the crowd was rough if Turk were with him. Although Bluford himself could be pretty tough, none of the rowdy boys wanted to tangle with Turk the giant. Thus, Turk was Bluford's unofficial bodyguard.

Bluford claimed to be Turk's "best friend;" but he had never "put Turk in a deal." It was common practice among the oil operators to allow some of their non-oil friends to buy interests in wells to be drilled. These participants joined the activity in total trust of the operator friend, never realizing they were accepting joint and several liability—the individual is legally liable for all debts of the group—for anything that went wrong, even though their interests might be miniscule.

In the early spring of 1961, Bluford, at last, had a proposition for Turk. "Turk, I'm going to put you in a deal. In fact, I'm going to drill the Stroud well in your name."

Bluford was not then, and never had been, an operator. However, he was deeply involved in the affairs of Carter-Jones Drilling Company, not as an owner; but as a participant in all the wells operated and drilled by Carter-Jones, many of which were illegally deviated. Bluford was speaking for Carter-Jones when he offered to put Turk in the deal. (Carter-Jones would actually be in charge of the drilling of the well; but the Railroad Commission would see "John George" listed as operator, the individual responsible for all operations.) Turk, of course, knew nothing about drilling an oil well; nor did he know that his friends were drilling illegally slanted holes to steal oil. Those activities were secrets freely discussed among the deviators, but only among them. Turk was as innocent as a babe in the woods.

So, Turk, the gentle giant who knew nothing about the oil patch (other than his Rail birds), was now an oil operator. He couldn't have been happier to claim he was finally an oilman.

Carter-Jones drilled the #4-A well on the W. H. Stroud lease in Rusk County in April of 1961. A later inclination survey showed the well deviated as much as 56 degrees from vertical, and contained 5,206 feet of pipe—all this in a well permitted for a depth of 3,500 feet. The bottom of the well was in Sun Oil's R. J. Hendon lease, 3,000 feet from the original surface location. Sun's legitimate wells on this lease were bottomed 3,500 feet from the surface.

The Investigating Committee subpoenaed Turk to appear at the first hearing in August 1962; but his attorney Fred Erisman advised him to remain silent. The Gregg County Grand Jury named him, along with 57 others, in its December 1962 indictments, charging him with grand theft.

A young attorney for Sun Oil called Turk and wanted to talk. Turk called his friend and fellow Lebanese, George Joseph (then a young field engineer who had recently started working the oil fields independently) for advice. George had an excellent reputation for his ability to find oil legitimately as well as for his honesty. He advised Turk to meet the Sun Oil attorney. George said he would be there at Turk's modest frame home on Glover Street as his backup during the interview.

The lawyer arrived in Longview at the appointed hour. He surveyed Turk's humble abode and immediately concluded that something was amiss. Turk was obviously not a high roller, unlike the other deviators. The lawyer studied Turk for a while; then he said, "Mr. George, you sure do look familiar. Don't I know you from somewhere?" It wasn't long before the young attorney figured out that Turk had been his baseball coach back in Tyler some fifteen years earlier. "Mr. George, it's clear to me that although you are listed as the operator of this well, you are not the real thief. Now, I don't have the authority to dismiss you from this lawsuit, but Sun will have one hell of a fight with me if they try to pursue you."

After the scandal had finally died down, Turk never spoke about it; he just carried on with work and harbored no ill will toward those who seduced him into the slant-hole affair. In his opinion, Big Oil had been the greedy parties who wanted to have the whole oil field to themselves.

Although Attorney General Wilson's civil penalty suits filed in the Travis County District Court resulted in judgments against several slant-holers, including Turk, neither the courts nor Sun Oil ever got a dime out of Turk.

I had met Turk shortly after my return to Longview, but I got to know him as a friend after my then wife and Turk's daughter Pat, who is Artistic Director of the Longview Ballet Theatre, became friends in 1986. While the two women were involved in ballet business, I often spent pleasant evenings with Turk, listening as he recounted the Normandy landing and Patton's march across Europe. Turk died just before the clock struck midnight on December 31, 1992.

CHAPTER 34
RITTER'S RECOLLECTIONS

Otto A. Ritter, a Longview lawyer, gave an oral history interview with Tommy L. Short, a Baylor University history student in 1973. (1). Ritter had represented several of the deviators when they were called to testify at the hearings held by the House General Investigating Committee in the late summer of 1962. His recollections of the slant-hole matter provide a perspective, if one-sided, of one who was intimately involved.

Ritter was born in the riverfront town of Jefferson in northeast Texas in 1920, and graduated from the public schools of nearby Marshall in 1938. After five years of active duty with the United States Air Force in the Pacific theater, Ritter left the military as a lieutenant colonel. After his return from the war, he attended East Texas Baptist College and Baylor Law School.

After receiving a law degree from Baylor in 1949, Ritter practiced law in Longview with the firm of Kenley, Sharp, and Ritter until 1965, when he formed his own law firm, Ritter, Nichols, Parker, and Thibodeaux. He was active in civic affairs in Longview as a founding director of the Good Shepherd Hospital, as a member of the Junior Chamber of Commerce and the Rotary Club, and as senior warden of the Trinity Episcopal Church.

Ritter was known in East Texas as an aggressive advocate and was generally disliked by the lawyers in East Texas. He even lost his temper during a trial in Henderson and was slugged by the opposing counsel.

Ritter described to Short how major oil companies encouraged and profited from the slant drilling.

It was and remains common practice for an independent operator to seek a farmout (sublease) of a portion of a lease owned by a major company. In such a legitimate transaction, the major company might determine that the little bit of oil in the undrilled portion of a lease would be unprofitable for its own production because of the major's high overhead expense. However, an independent with far less overhead could make a profit from marginal wells (those that could produce only a few barrels per day).

The major oil companies owned most of the leases along the eastern edge of the field, many of which extended beyond the eastern productive limit. A major company, according to Ritter, would offer an independent operator a farmout on the unproductive portion of such a lease and retain a one-eighth interest in the production, if any. In making the deal, the oil company's negotiator would respond to the independent's complaint that no oil existed beneath the land being offered, "Well, you go ahead and drill it there and you bottom your hole wherever you want to and nobody's going to say anything." The result of the trade was a well slanted from outside the limit of the field back into the productive oil zone. The major company got one-eighth of the income from the production without risk or cost, making the lease provide the major more income than it was entitled to receive.

The major companies bought the oil produced from these farmouts because they owned the refineries, and their field men, according to Ritter, knew of the illicit activity although the corporate officers did not.

After the major companies had filed lawsuits against the deviators, several companies laid off employees or forced many of their field men to take early retirement. The men affected by these acts resented their dismissals. Ritter claimed he got this information from such an employee of a major company during a lawsuit against his client. Now that the field men were unemployed, they informed lawyers, but not necessarily the Ranger investigators, of their former employers' complicity in the slant-hole matter.

In the interview, Ritter—Judge Sharp's law partner for a dozen years until 1965—described the deteriorating relationship between Sharp and Attorney General Will Wilson.

Property taxes provide the primary support for the public schools of Texas. Until the Peveto law went into effect in 1982, each taxing unit had set its own value on each property within its district. A property could have a different taxable value for each of the county, the city, the school district, and other entities. Generally, the county judge served as arbiter in disputes of value.

The Peveto Bill of 1978 established central appraisal districts in each county. Each appraisal district is charged to appraise all taxable property

within its county at 100 percent of fair market value. The law requires
all taxing units within the county to use the corresponding appraisal
district's value in setting tax rates. (2)

The major oil companies owned most of the oil production in the
East Texas Oil Field, as well as in nearby fields. Every year, they sent
representatives seeking to reduce the new values of their leases to Judge
Sharp. The most common justification for such reduction was that
the volume of oil remaining in the reservoir after the previous year's
production had decreased, leaving less oil to be produced. Sharp denied
most of these requests, and these denials led to hard feelings between
the oil companies and the judge. I have been told separately that Judge
Sharp was not always gentle in his denying the tax relief sought. The oil
companies, therefore, did not like Judge Sharp.

In his interview, Ritter said, "Because of the fact that he couldn't be
bought, he couldn't be intimidated, he was not going to let them off the
hook of their just, legal responsibilities."

Ritter also said that in 1961 Sharp had represented a group that
sought a state bank charter in Longview. Approval of such a charter
required the signatures of the governor, the attorney general, and the
banking commissioner—Price Daniel, Will Wilson, and J. M. Falkner,
respectively. Personal relations between Sharp and Daniel, who had been
classmates in law school, and between another unnamed attorney and
Wilson, helped Sharp's clients obtain the new bank's charter.

Daniel decided, against the advice of his friend and supporter Sharp,
to run in 1962 for a fourth two-year term as governor in a field of six
candidates that included Attorney General Wilson. Sharp had agreed,
however, to support Daniel if he did run. Ritter said, "Wilson thought
that people he helped get a charter ought to help him be elected governor
and called on Mr. Sharp to support him." Sharp explained to Wilson that
he and Daniel had been friends and classmates at Baylor Law School and
that he was bound to support his friend. Sharp further told Wilson that
he (Sharp) would support him (Wilson) if his (Sharp's) friend Daniel
were not running.

In the Democratic primary election held in May 1962, Daniel polled
third and Wilson fourth, behind John Connally and Don Yarborough. In

this loss (his first political defeat), Wilson was infuriated with Sharp for his lack of support. Both Sharp and Ritter had supported Wilson in his earlier campaigns for attorney general.

It was around this time when Sharp's slant-hole activity became known. Sharp had recently denied the major oil companies tax relief "... so Will Wilson took on the job of being a hatchet man for the oil companies," according to Ritter.

Ritter continued by saying:

Will Wilson persuaded a Grand Jury—he violated every rule in the book—went into the Grand Jury and demanded that they indict Earl Sharp.

[...] I'd say 99.9 percent of every indictment that Will Wilson had in Wood County and Gregg County and Rusk County, where he went into the Grand Jury room, and made a hell-fire and brimstone speech and got people indicted...none of them were ever convicted.

[...]

Because it was strictly a Kangaroo Court process. He did this with people who had been friends and some political but social friends all of his life and it was so raw that one of his closest friends and chums in college and law school made the remark at one of the hearings that he hated to see Will Wilson become so ambitious and that when he died they'd probably have to hire pallbearers.

[...]

That's how low the man went in people's esteem because of the unfair tactics that he followed.

Sharp had planned to run for re-election to the judgeship he had held since 1947, but according to Ritter, the majors wanted Sharp defeated. They got their wish. Peppy Blount, a hero of World War II, a football star at the University of Texas, and a former state legislator, ran a three-day write-in campaign and defeated Sharp with 55 percent of the vote on November 6.

The Wood County Grand Jury indicted Sharp on November 1, and the Gregg County Grand Jury indicted him on December 11. He resigned his office on November 12 and recommended that Blount be installed immediately. Instead, the court appointed Hamp Smead Jr. to finish Sharp's term, and Blount assumed office in January 1963.

Ritter claimed that Blount's performance as county judge was sub-par. He served only one term, through 1966. Henry Atkinson, whom I knew well, and who served as Gregg County judge between 1967 and 1990, said of Sharp, "He was a brilliant man and a brilliant lawyer, and he exercised great care in running the county from the administrative standpoint and kept up with his business as the judge as no one else could."(2)

On a side note, Blount's in-laws owned property on the eastern edge of the East Texas Oil Field on which several slanted wells produced illegal oil, without the knowledge or complicity of Blount or his wife, both of whom were friends of mine.

Sharp died at age 88 on June 26, 1999. Blount died on June 22, 2010, at 85.

NOTES

1. Otto Ritter, interview by Tommy L. Short, April 20, 1973, in Longview, Texas, transcript, Baylor University Institute for Oral History, Waco, TX, copyright 1974 by Baylor University; available online at: http://digitalcollections.baylor.edu/cdm/compoundobject/collection/buioh/id/1442/rec/3.
2. I served as a director of the Gregg County Central Appraisal District, 1990 – 1994.
3. Jo Lee Ferguson, *The Longview Morning Journal*, June 27, 1999.

CHAPTER 35
SOME THINGS NEVER CHANGE

If leopards never change their spots, some deviators don't either. Take the case of Bull Barber, who drilled his Goyne well into Shell's Laird well in April 1961. (Chapter 13)

One of Barber's acquaintances told me that Bull had many friends in high places, and that he sold used cars for his brother's Ford dealership in Overton. The story is that after computer-based accounting systems became available in the early 1980s, Barber made extra money when his brother converted his bookkeeping from a manual system to a computer system. Barber used the month-long conversion process to sell a record number of cars at whatever price he could get, but Ford never heard about his big sales during that month.

In 1979, a local rancher spotted a suspicious truck hooked to an oil storage tank near Longview shortly before midnight. (1) He reported his observation to the Railroad Commission (the Kilgore office ?), which commenced an investigation. (2) Bull and his son, Bradford S. (in 2008, Buddy) were among 16 persons indicted by the Gregg County Grand Jury on March 9, 1981, as Gregg County District Attorney Rob Foster said, "under the organized crime statute and alleges [sic] a conspiracy to form a combination for profit to commit the crime of theft over $10,000." The specific "offense involved hauling stolen oil from an oil field to a refinery where it was sold." (3) Commission employee Clint Garner testified that he "was offered $1 a barrel for every barrel of stolen oil from an East Texas field if he would disclose the location of law enforcement patrols" and "said he was told that could bring him 'at least $5,000' a month." Garner "said Buddy Barber told him he would pay him for information about the locations of agents and explained, 'We have got to move hot oil out of the East Texas field.'" The same *Times* article said, "an oil field pumper testified that he was paid $2 for every barrel of oil stolen after he left a security gate unlocked on specified nights." (4) Recall that the price of oil had spiked to $30 per barrel in response to the overthrow of the Shah by adherents of Ayatollah Khomeini in 1979. Thus, the bribes noted amounted to only 10 percent of the value of the stolen oil.

A Longview jury found Bull, Buddy, and Mrs. Jean Brown of Oklahoma guilty of conspiring to steal oil from an East Texas oil field on June 30, 1982. (5) The convicted elected to have the judge (Marcus Vascocu) assess the sentences, which would range from five to 99 years or life in prison, plus a fine of up to $10,000." Each of them pleaded for mercy owing to health problems; but the prosecutor said of Bull, "It's his problem. But what he does with other people's oil is the business of this court, and the business of the jury. We have three people who thought they could just thumb their nose [sic] at the law." Judge Vascocu sentenced each of the three to five years in prison along with fines of $5,000 for each on July 13, 1982. (6) The defendants appealed their convictions to the Court of Appeals in Texarkana, which overturned the convictions on February 21, 1984 (7) ; but the Texas Court of Criminal Appeals, the last level for appeals of criminal cases, reversed the Texarkana court and affirmed the trial court's convictions on December 7, 1988. (8), (9) Then, the high court reversed itself and overturned the convictions in 1991. (10) I found no evidence that either of the Barbers spent any time in jail.

Kenneth C. Miller was a Tyler oilman who died in 1974 leaving a multi-million-dollar estate. A special grand jury in Smith County indicted three men citing conspiracies over a period of three years during which the three are alleged to have "milked assets" from the Miller estate. Among the three were Kenneth Wayne Goodwin, son of Ben Goodwin, the co-trustee with RepublicBank, of the estate, and Bull Barber. The charges against Barber were second degree theft, third degree theft, and conspiracy to commit second degree theft. (11), (12)

Buddy Barber found himself in police custody on September 24, 1985, having been named in a sealed indictment returned Sept. 18. It charged him with criminal conspiracy in the burning of the East Texas Lumber Company on February 16. At press time, three of the other defendants had already pleaded guilty, but a Gregg County jury found Buddy not guilty. (13), (14)

Bull Barber died at age 79 in 1998, and his son Buddy died in 2008. (15), (16)

NOTES

1. "3 convicted in Etex oil thefts," *The Times* (Shreveport), July 1, 1982, p. 1.

2. "FBI Enters Manhunt," *Tyler Morning Telegraph*, March 20, 1981, p. 10.

3. Jerry Graham, "Gregg, Rusk residents nabbed today," *The Longview News-Journal*, March 12, 1981, p.1.

4. See Note 1.

5. "Three Convicted In Oil Conspiracy," *Tyler Morning Telegraph*, July 1, 1982, p. 14.

6. Jerry Graham, "Three 'hot oil' defendants get jail time, fine," *The Longview News-Journal*, July 14, 1982, pp.1, 15.

7. Barber v. State, 668 S.W. 2d 424 (Tex. App.-Texarkana (1984).

8. Barber v. State, 764 S. W.2d 232 (Tex. Crim. App.1988).

9. Wire Reports, "Appeals Court Upholds Convictions of ET Residents In 'Hot Oil' Deal," *Tyler Morning Telegraph*, December 8, 1988, p. 7.

10. Jerry Graham, "Hot oil case convictions overturned," *Longview News-Journal*, January 31, 1991, p. 2.

11. "East Texans named in indictments," *The Longview News-Journal*, March 28, 1985, p. 15.

12. Doug Cooper, "3 ETexans Indicted In Oil Estate Probe," *Tyler Morning Telegraph*, March 28, 1985, p. 1.

13. "Kilgore Man Arrested In East Texas Company Fire," *Tyler Courier Times*, September 25, 1985, p. 8.

14. "Jury Finds Kilgore Man Not Guilty In Arson Case," *Tyler Morning Courier*, January 16, 1986, p.5.

15. "Kilgore Services Friday For W. S. 'Bull' Barber," *Tyler Morning Telegraph*, August 6, 1998, p. 14.

16. Bradford Stanley Barber, obituary, *The Longview News-Journal*, April 28, 2008, p.8.

EPILOGUE

Many of my friends asked me why I wanted to stir up an old controversy by writing this book 50 years after the events. Most wanted me to let sleeping dogs lie. Too many people will be embarrassed to see their family names associated with the scandal, they said. I even encountered some threats, warning me not to write and publish the story.

I wrote this book because I wanted to provide a detailed case study of a grand theft that involved hundreds of individuals and rocked the State of Texas in the early 1960s. I have explained here how otherwise good men, and some not so good, allowed greed to overcome good judgment and justify thievery. These men took advantage of East Texas geology and state laws that made the theft inevitable. I have explained how ordinary East Texans got revenge for what they saw as Big Oil's maltreatment of their ancestors and their friends. I do not intend, however, to justify their theft of millions of barrels of oil, even if I understand their resentment toward Big Oil.

I have shown here that those who drilled the crooked wells could not have succeeded for 17 years without the collusion of several employees of the Railroad Commission. But accusations against the commissioners were never proved nor, apparently, even seriously investigated. An indictment in 1963 of Chairman Bill Murray was dismissed. The well-servicing companies, whose jobs included surveying and logging each well when drilled, swore to false documents and used the U.S. mail for their delivery, a federal crime. Local law enforcement officials turned a blind eye to events they knew about—and in which some even participated.

The events of the slant-hole affair came about only because no one involved had the courage to say no. Some oilmen in East Texas avoided participation, but not many.

When I asked some living deviators or their survivors why they got involved, the typical response was, "Well, everybody else was doing it."

But the guilt of others did not excuse the deviators. There are no heroes in this story. Most, if not all of the deviators, were men of substantial means who had no need to resort to theft for financial support. But once so many had joined the thefts, it was too late, and the chain of deceit took on a life of its own.

This scandal differs from other infamous events in detail, but not in kind. The sums of money involved, the timing, and the vehicles for theft are different, as are the numbers of people affected. The complicity of legislators and regulators bought by or for the perpetrators is a common thread in all thefts of this kind.

No one can be proud of this story; that's probably why others have never told it in full.

The consequences of the scandal did not sit lightly with some of the participants. Some lived with guilt and shame. Some felt the sting of gossip of former friends. In many cases, children and grandchildren are still unaware of their granddaddy's involvement. Many have been reluctant to reveal the family secret in the hope that younger descendants won't find out. I sympathize with them, but I know that every family has its share of wayward ancestors, including mine.

Some of the deviators and/or their children, however, continue to get together and review the events of the scandal, almost in celebration of their having gotten away with their escapades. They showed Big Oil they would not be forever mistreated without consequence. I have participated in some of these gatherings. That's where I learned some of what I have told here.

The slant-hole story remains an important part of Texas history, and it has been mentioned in print only superficially. (1-5) I have tried here to tell the whole story clearly with enough detail and documentation to be credible, but without overburdening the reader with excess detail. I added some of my own comments when I felt it made the story clearer.

I have been told by some individuals that some of the slanted wells remain undetected and are still producing to this day. These individuals would not, however, tell me where the wells are. I met a man one afternoon at the commission's Kilgore office who told me his "business was plugging abandoned wells and that he had just plugged a deviated well that day. When all of the deviated wells are finally plugged and abandoned, I doubt the removal of excess tubing will be recorded. There will be no trace of these wells."

APPENDIX - Slant-Hole Indictments by County

	County	Upshur	Gregg	Gregg	Rusk	Wood	Gregg	Wood	Total
	Date Returned	10/3/62	10/22/62	10/26/62	11/9/62	11/1/62	12/11/62	2/6/63	Counts
1	Adams, Ewing					4			4
2	Allgood, Reid					3	2		5
3	Baker, Don L.		1				1		2
4	Barber, W. S. "Bull"				1				1
5	Baton, J.W.					2			2
6	Bissell, Harry	1					1		2
7	Bialack, Joe						2		2
8	Brock, M.C.						2		2
9	Cargill, Robert				1		1		2
10	Christopher, Charles						2		2
11	Clark, Max						2		2
12	Cook, Tom Jr.				1		2		3
13	Davis, W.O. Jr.				1		2		3
14	Davis, Pete	1							1
15	Decker, Nelson		15				2		17

	County	Upshur	Gregg	Gregg	Rusk	Wood	Gregg	Wood	Total
	Date Returned	10/3/62	10/22/62	10/26/62	11/9/62	11/1/62	12/11/62	2/6/63	Counts
16	Deutsch, F.C.	1							1
17	Deutsch, W.C.	1							1
18	Gaumer, Daryl R.				1		2		3
19	Gibson, Leon					2			2
20	Godfrey, Douglas					2		2	4
21	Green, C.C.						2		2
22	Hallmark, B.J.		2				1		3
23	Harrington, H.M. Jr.					6	2		8
24	Hearn, E.B. Jr.				1		2		3
25	Hearn, E.B. Sr.				2			2	4
26	Hedge, Raymond						2		2
27	Henderson, W.R.				1			6	7
28	Hewell, W.A.	1							1
29	Hobbs, M.X.						2		2

#	County / Date Returned	Upshur 10/3/62	Gregg 10/22/62	Gregg 10/26/62	Rusk 11/9/62	Wood 11/1/62	Gregg 12/11/62	Wood 2/6/63	Total Counts
30	Hobbs, W.H.		1	1	1		2		5
31	Jones, Harry C.		2		2	1	2		7
32	Jordan, G.M.		3	1	1				5
33	Laird, J.D.				2		2		4
34	Long, H.L. (Pete)				1		1		2
35	Lutes, Charles W.		1	2		6	3		12
36	Massad, Ralph					2			2
37	Matthews, Robert W.	1	2	1					4
38	Maxwell, J.K.		2		2	1	22		27
39	Maxwell, W.T.		2		2	1	22		27
40	McCubbin, A.E. (Jack)		3		1		22		26
41	McCubbin, J.S.						16		16
42	Medley, R.S.						4		4
43	Mitchell, W.E. Jr.	1					3		4
44	Moore, David C.							1	1

	County	Upshur	Gregg	Gregg	Rusk	Wood	Gregg	Wood	Total
	Date Returned	10/3/62	10/22/62	10/26/62	11/9/62	11/1/62	12/11/62	2/6/63	Counts
45	Murphy, L. Dwight	3	18		1	1	8		33
46	Orr, B.B.							3	3
47	Owens, R.E.		1						1
48	Patton, J.L.						5		5
49	Powell, L.W.						4	1	5
50	Scates, E.W.	3	1		2		3		9
51	Sharp, Earl					3	2		5
52	Snider, C.J.							2	2
53	Snider, Joe							2	2
54	Starr, C.S.	1					1		2
55	Stegall, Rex				1		22		23
56	Teer, Gerald		1				1		2
57	Thomas, Owen				1		4		5
58	Tyner, J.W.	1	8	1		1	5		16
59	Vaughan, Arthur	1					1		2
60	Walker, J.G.					5			5
61	Walker, W.C.						2		2
62	Wrather, John E.						1		1

County	Upshur	Gregg	Gregg	Rusk	Wood	Gregg	Wood	Total
Date Returned	10/3/62	10/22/62	10/26/62	11/9/62	11/1/62	12/11/62	2/6/63	Counts
63 Yoachum, G.U.		8	8			15		31
Total # Counts/Grand Jury	16	71	16	26	36	209	18	392
	FWST 10/4/62	GCGJ RPT	FWST 10/27/62	FWST 11/11/62	DMN 11/2/62	GCGJ RPT	DMN 2/9/63	
					FWST 11/2/62	DMN 12/12/62		

Key: (FWST) *Fort Worth Star-Telegram*; (DMN) *The Dallas Morning News*; (GCGJ RPT) Gregg County Grand Jury Report

ACKNOWLEDGMENTS

Writing this book first occurred to me in 1980, when I learned that Pat Smith, who had died four years earlier, had collected and cataloged some 300 newspaper articles from the 1960s about the slant-hole affair. Pat had been a lobbyist for my father for nearly 20 years. He had also possessed a copy of the Texas House General Investigating Committee's report that contained his written comments on the hearings that took place in the 1960s. And he had also possessed photographs of the dedication of the Boy Scout well that were taken on January 14, 1949. Pat's collection was in my father's possession and became mine when I returned to Texas to join my father's business in 1980. I became serious about writing the story after I was comfortable with my transition from academic scientist to businessman—a process that took about 10 years. My first thanks, therefore, go to Pat Smith for preserving the history that would have been long buried had it not been for his foresight.

My office colleagues helped me sift through my mother's newspaper clippings and those of Faye Bradley, the widow of a Railroad Commission engineer, to find a few golden nuggets. I give my thanks to my late mother, and to the late Mrs. Bradley, for these newspaper articles, and I also offer thanks to Brandy Scott Bonner, Rachel Cummings Briley, and Amanda Koepke for their organizing and summarizing the articles.

Thanks to Stefani Wrightman for organizing the tables of slanted wells and indictments.

Thanks to Charla Rolf of the Texas Railroad Commission's Kilgore office, and later, her own oil field reporting service, for guiding me through the commission's Byzantine records system. I could never have located the files for many slanted wells without her guidance.

Ms. Kay Cook helped me in my search of the Throckmorton County records for the details of the Bill Murray oil deals that brought him down.

with information from their books and records, and agreed to allow me to quote extensively from them.

Personal interviews with Robert Allgood, Gore Kemp, Jo Maxwell, Bill Maxwell, Emily Erisman Meyers, Pat George Mitchell, James Moore, Risa Ray, Linward Shivers, Archie Tehan, Rob Foster, and John David Wrather provided numerous insights into the details of the scandal. Thanks to each of them.

Thanks to Tom Perryman, who gave me a copy of his recording of the closing arguments in the trial of Humble v. Long discussed in Chapter 7. Tom was a good friend until his death on January 11, 2018.

Special thanks to the late Ranger Glenn Elliott for sharing his insight into the slant-hole matter, but many more thanks for his personal example and for his 50 years of deep friendship with my family. Glenn passed away in 2012 on New Year's Eve, leaving a big hole in the lives of all who knew, loved, and respected him.

Many thanks to my executive assistant, Janine Briley, without whom I could not have assembled this story. Her encouragement, her organizational abilities, and her records management expertise helped make it all happen. After Janine's retirement, Marianne Edwards continued to be my right hand. She has been invaluable in this effort, as well.

To those who patiently suffered the assaults and demands upon our friendship and who read and commented on numerous drafts of chapters in this book, I cannot extend adequate thanks: William C. Agosta, my longtime friend; Martha, my beloved wife; William and Tom, my sons; and Hope Butterworth, my daughter, and Bonnie Granat, my copyeditor who made me clarify the oil field jargon and made me write complete sentences..

The Mayborn Conference on Nonfiction Writing, sponsored by the Mayborn School of Journalism at the University of North Texas, brought me in contact with fellow aspiring writers and successful writers, agents, and coaches, all of whom made a significant contribution to the book you now hold. I am forever grateful to all the Mayborn Tribe, especially George Getschow, Roy Busby, Dorothy Bland, and Susannah Charleson, for encouraging me to get this book finished and published. I met Ben Fountain at the 2019 Mayborn Conference. He encouraged my writing and introduced me to David Abrams, who edited the present version of this book.

Without the Dallas Public Library's searchable database of *The Dallas Morning News*, I would have never been able to document much of what I report here. I shall forever be grateful to the City of Dallas for the gift of this great library.

Big thanks to Amanda Masterson of the Bureau of Economic Geology (BEG) at the University of Texas at Austin for arranging permission to use materials from a BEG publication; to Glenn McCutchen, former publisher of *The Longview News-Journal*, for permission to include a complete story from that newspaper; Thanks also to Rusty Bloxom of the Texas Rangers Hall of Fame and Museum, Waco, Texas, for photos of Rangers Bob Crowder and Jim Ray, as well as for making it possible for me to spend three days in December 2018 reviewing the Rangers' files on the slant-hole affair at the Rangers Museum.

Others, too numerous to count, and especially Dr. John Parker and Whitney Schaap, provided encouragement and advice for which I am deeply grateful.

My wife, Martha, read, corrected, and reread most of this book and made many suggestions for its improvement, but her main contribution was her belief in me and in the project. Without her love, encouragement, and patience, I could not have written this story.

CPSIA information can be obtained
at www.ICGtesting.com
Printed in the USA
JSHW022223210621
16109JS00002B/9

9 781622 884025